Basic
Car Maintenance
and Repairs

by Paul Weissler

Drawings by
Lloyd Birmingham

POPULAR SCIENCE

HARPER & ROW

New York, Evanston, San Francisco, London

Contents

Preface

With the purchase of this book you are on your way to becoming a weekend auto mechanic. You won't have to wait weeks for service appointments, pay high prices for labor and list prices for parts. And the job will be done right the first time, because it's your car and you care.

Certainly you're a bit apprehensive. You may have looked under the hood of your car a dozen times and thought, "I wish I could fix it myself." The truth is that you can't do everything, but there are many routine jobs on a car that you can do—without a major investment in special tools and equipment. These are the jobs that millions of other motorists have discovered require no special training, no "mechanical aptitude"—nothing but a willingness to follow simple instructions.

If you are willing to try, the potential savings are enormous. Just doing the basic maintenance jobs explained in Chapter 3 would save you $270 over a five-year period. Chapters 6 and 7, covering tune-up, can save you an additional $225 over the same period. The two-car family with a do-it-yourselfer could save almost $1000.

To make it easy for you to break into do-it-yourself auto mechanics, this book has been prepared with these features:

• Explanations are step-by-step and profusely illustrated, not only with drawings but "in-the-metal" photographs on actual cars.

• Cautionary notes are included where the beginner might make a mistake.

• Special help is given for the problems a beginner might otherwise consider insurmountable.

You should approach do-it-yourself auto maintenance with a high degree of confidence. Well over 50 percent of the cars in this country get the do-it-yourself maintenance described in Chapter 6. More than 30 percent are tuned by a member of the owning family. Department stores throughout the United States carry an enormous range of automotive parts, in response to what they have found is a huge retail market.

The professional mechanic spends his day trying to turn out as many jobs as possible. He may forget to tighten a spark plug, he may leave out a washer, among an assortment of other errors. You have only your car to service. If you take the care he can't, you will save money and have confidence and pride in your work.

1 | Getting Acquainted with Your Car

We're all more comfortable in familiar surroundings. If you become familiar with what is under the hood and the body of your car, you can approach repair and maintenance work with confidence. When you look at the many different parts, don't worry about them all. You must learn to zero in on the ones that require service. Every engine compartment is crammed with so many parts that most professional mechanics would be unable to name them all. Indeed, there are so many wires and hoses, sealed little electrical components, emission control devices, and other obscure parts that most factory engineers can't identify them all without reference manuals. This doesn't frighten the professional mechanic, and it shouldn't bother you. Learn to look for the specific items you're concerned about and "tune out" the rest.

RAISING THE HOOD. The first thing you must learn is how to release, lift up, and support the hood. Don't be embarrassed if it takes a while to figure that out; many service station attendants who lift hoods all day struggle over one with which they're unfamiliar.

If you have an owner's manual for your car, check it for instructions. Lost the manual? Then, begin by looking for a knob, usually T-shaped, under the dashboard, to the left of your left knee when you're in driving position (Fig. 1-1). If

1-1.   Some hood releases are inside the car. This one is plainly marked.

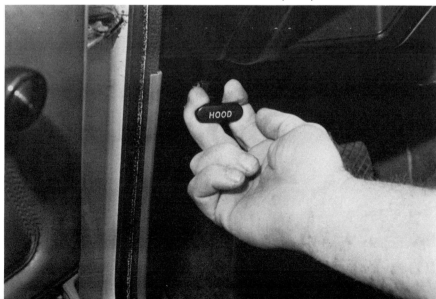

the knob pulls out easily, and you don't hear the hood pop open, it's a vent control, not a hood release. The hood control is probably at the front of the car, as it is on most American automobiles.

At the front of the car, using a flashlight, look for a latch you can pull, lift, or push to one side. On many cars it is at the top or bottom of the grille. On some cars it is under the front bumper. (See Figs. 1-2 and 1-3.)

Once you operate the latch, the hood will pop partly open, but you still won't be able to lift it, because it will be held by a safety catch. There are two possible ways the safety catch can be released:

(1) You may again operate the main latch, holding it in the "open" position as far as possible, then lift up the hood. This arrangement is commonly used on cars with latch controls under the bumper.

(2) There is a safety catch lever at the hood release itself and once the hood pops partly open, you'll see it. Note: you may have to push down slightly on the hood as you operate the lever, in order for the safety catch to release.

Most hoods are self-supporting in the raised position, by means of heavy springs at the rear. Others have to be held up by a rod which fits in a slot in the hood. Be sure to engage the rod in the slot so the hood won't fall when you're working underneath.

1-2. This hood release is in the grille-work. Just reach in for it.

1-3. T-handle hood release is under front bumper.

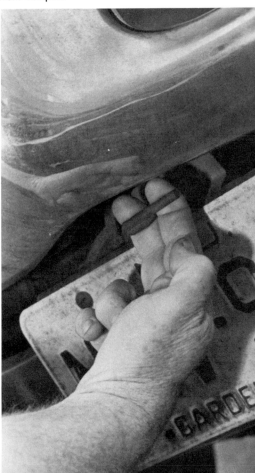

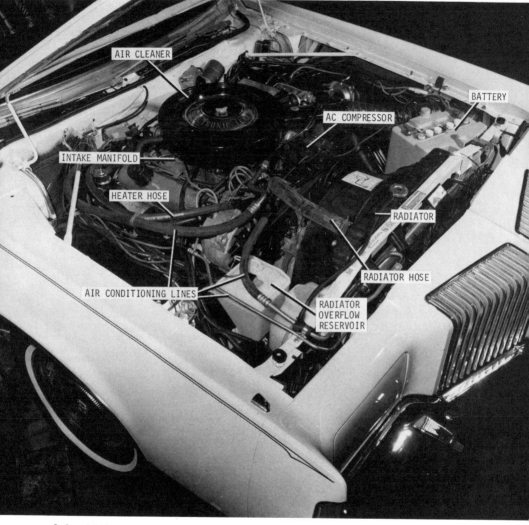

1-4. A V-8 engine compartment with some key parts identified. Notice that air conditioning lines follow a similar path to heater hose for part of engine compartment but then continue to the air conditioning compressor. The heater hose connects to the engine.

THE ENGINE COMPARTMENT. The engine compartment of a late-model car certainly is a busy-looking place. Figs. 1-4 through 1-7 show some typical engines and engine compartments so you can get oriented. Let's take a tour through the compartment, and if you have the hood of your own car or cars raised at the same time, you'll see many of the same things "in the metal."

A good place to start is at the **air cleaner**. That's the big cannister in the top center, with a cover held by a wingnut. Inside is a filter (Fig. 1-8), made of specially treated pleated paper.

Your engine runs on a mixture of gasoline and air, and it is the filter that removes abrasive particles from that air—particles that could damage the engine.

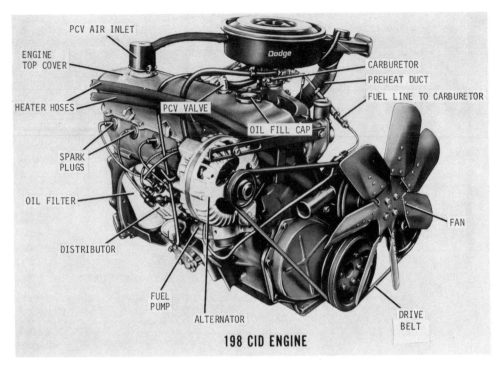

PCV AIR INLET

ENGINE
TOP COVER

HEATER HOSES

PCV VALVE

OIL FILL CAP

SPARK
PLUGS

OIL FILTER

DISTRIBUTOR

FUEL
PUMP

ALTERNATOR

CARBURETOR

PREHEAT DUCT

FUEL LINE TO CARBURETOR

FAN

DRIVE
BELT

198 CID ENGINE

1-5. Two views of this six-cylinder engine show many parts, some of which will be discussed in future chapters. The driver's side view, although of the same basic engine, is actually of a different model. Note the antipollution air pump.

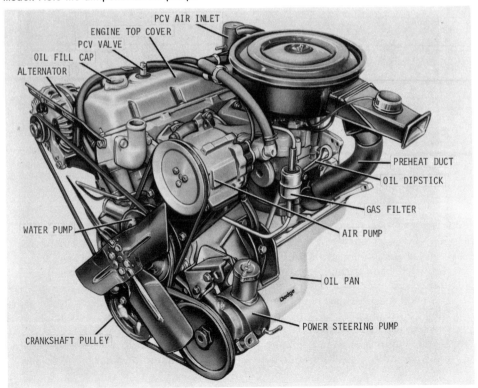

PCV AIR INLET

ENGINE TOP COVER

PCV VALVE

OIL FILL CAP

ALTERNATOR

PREHEAT DUCT

OIL DIPSTICK

GAS FILTER

AIR PUMP

WATER PUMP

OIL PAN

OIL PAN

POWER STEERING PUMP

CRANKSHAFT PULLEY

1-6. This view of a V-8 shows that each side has its own engine top cover, and that the intake manifold is placed between the sides of the V. Observe the oil filter, which can be located almost anywhere on the lower part of an engine.

The mixing is done in a component the air cleaner sits on—the **carburetor.** Look underneath the air cleaner as you have someone step on the gas pedal, and you'll see linkage move at the carburetor. This linkage controls a part called the throttle, which regulates the amount of air-fuel mix that can flow through the carburetor. The carburetor is mounted on the **intake manifold,** a part with chambers that carries fuel mixture into the engine. Burned gases are carried out of the engine through another part with chambers, the exhaust manifold, from which they flow into exhaust piping and the muffler.

1-7. Top view of six-cylinder engine compartment shows routing of heater hose (easy to see on a car without air conditioning), upper radiator hose, oil fill cap, and battery.

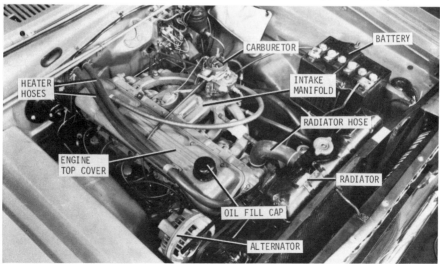

1-8. Air filter, made of pleated paper, sits in a housing that has a removable cover.

Next, look at the front of the engine and you'll see a lot of pulleys with belts wrapped around them. The components with these pulleys are operated by power transferred from the engine via the belts.

The power source is at the lowest pulley, which is bolted to the engine's crankshaft, and as the crankshaft turns, it spins its pulley, and the belts wrapped around it, sending some power out to other pulleys. Among components given power by pulleys and belts are:

Alternator (an AC generator). It converts mechanical energy from the engine into electrical energy, and by wires sends that electricity to the car's battery and electrically operated components, such as the radio, lights, etc.

Power steering pump. The spinning pulley operates a fluid pump that sends oil under pressure to the steering gear, to help you turn the steering wheel. It is the component with the two hoses to the housing at the front end of the steering column. It has a fluid reservoir at the top, with a cap that has a built-in measuring stick (called a dipstick) to permit checking the fluid level.

Water pump. This is a pulley-operated fluid pump that circulates the water-antifreeze mixture through the engine to absorb heat. It pulls the hot coolant from the engine and pumps it into the component that dissipates the heat into the air—the radiator. The water pump typically can be identified by the fan mounted on its front.

Air-conditioning compressor. This is a pulley-operated pump that circulates a special gas, called refrigerant, throughout the airconditioning system. The compressor draws refrigerant that has absorbed heat from the passenger compartment (cooling it) and pumps it into the condenser, which dissipates it. The condenser is mounted just in front of the radiator. You can identify the compressor by the fact that one of the tubes connected to it also goes to the condenser.

Air pump. Many but not all late-models cars are equipped with a pulley-operated air pump, which draws in outside air, compresses it, and transmits it through tubing into parts of the car's exhaust system. This is an anti-pollution device designed to supply extra air to consume particles of unburned fuel before they escape from the exhaust system into the atmosphere. In most cases the belt that operates this pump also drives other belt-powered accessories. In some cases the pump is operated by a belt solely from the power-steering pump, which has a double pulley, one for the belt from the crankshaft, the other for the belt to the air pump. This pump normally can be identified by the single rubber hose from its housing.

Next, look for the **ignition distributor** (Fig. 1-9). The distributor does exactly what its name implies—it takes high-voltage electricity created in the ignition coil and distributes it to the spark plugs, one at a time, through wires that are connected to it at one end, and to the plugs at the other. The electricity "fires" the spark plugs, which are threaded into the engine, and the firing causes the air-fuel mixture to explode, creating power.

Once you have found the distributor, you can easily locate other key parts of the system that fires the plugs, called the *ignition system*. The thick wires on top of the distributor, in the part called the cap, lead to the spark plugs, so you can locate the plugs just by following them. On all but 1975 and later General Motors cars with V-8 engines (and a few with four-cylinder engines) there is an extra wire that leads to the ignition coil. On the GM cars mentioned, the coil is built into the distributor cap.

1-9.   Side view of an in-line six-cylinder engine shows key ignition system parts.

Now, let's identify the key parts of the *cooling system*. In front of the water pump and fan is the rectangular part with all the fins, which dissipates the heat into the air. That's the **radiator**. It has one hose on top, another on the bottom that fits into a neck on the water pump.

The water pump is now worth a closer inspection. In addition to the hose from the radiator, there is a second hose of perhaps one inch in outer diameter also connected to it—that's the outlet hose from the heater. If you follow that hose it will go to the rear of the engine compartment and line up with a second hose of the same diameter (or reasonably close), the heater inlet hose. Follow the heater inlet hose and it will go to the top of the engine, perhaps into a valve assembly.

Finding the car's storage box for electrical energy—the **battery**—should be no problem. The battery has two thick cables (wires) connected to it. Follow them both.

One will eventually wind its way to a terminal at the back of the engine, onto the **starter motor**. The other likely is split into two wires, one that is attached to the body sheet metal, a second that is bolted to the engine.

On some cars, primarily Ford products and certain American Motors cars, the cable to the starter is a two-piece design, one from the battery to a part called a relay, a second from the relay to the starter. The relay is a type of switch, controlled by current from the dashboard ignition key. When you turn the key, you close a dashboard switch that sends current to the relay, operating an electromagnet that closes a switch in the relay and permitting current to flow from battery to starter. The majority of cars, which are not equipped with this relay, have a starter that incorporates a part called a solenoid, which, among other jobs, performs a similar function.

THE ENGINE. Most of the work that you will perform on the car will not actually be done on the engine itself, but on parts and accessories attached to it. However, a general familiarity with the layout of the engine is useful, and there are a few parts of the engine with which you should be familiar.

First are the **oil dipstick** and the **oil filler cap**. The dipstick, which measures the level of oil in the engine, is a long steel rod with a handle that fits into a tube attached to the engine. When looking for the dipstick on cars with automatic transmission, you must be careful, for there are two dipsticks, one for the engine, one for the transmission. The one with the larger diameter tube is for the transmission, and it should clearly be to the rear of the one for engine oil.

The oil filler cap is the part you remove to add oil to the engine. It is normally on the sheet-metal cover on top of the engine (there are two such covers on a V-8), and it should be on one of them. Or it may be on a long pipe from the engine. The location should be obvious, but if not, watch a service station attendant the next time you buy a quart of oil.

THE UNDERBODY. Let's continue the tour with a look at the car's underbody. To raise the car safely so you can get underneath, you need ramps or a special jack and safety stands. (See Chapter 2, Tools for Servicing Your Car.) *Caution:* Do not use the bumper jack that comes with the car. It is meant only to lift the car sufficiently to remove a wheel, and is not secure enough to permit crawling underneath.

The underside of the car is a dark place, so take a large flashlight or spotlamp with you.

DRAIN PLUG

1-10. Oil drain plug looks like a bolt threaded into the oil pan.

First, look for the engine's **oil pan**, which is the oil reservoir into which the end of the dipstick fits. On most cars it is a sheet-metal pan held by many screws. *Note*: On cars with automatic transmission you should notice two pans, one at the front of the car, the other toward the center, approximately under the front part of the passenger compartment. The front pan, which is between the two front wheels, is the engine oil pan, and at a low point you should see a **drain plug**. It resembles a bolt that isn't holding anything (Fig. 1-10). When the engine oil is changed, this plug is removed to drain the old oil.

Next, notice the exhaust system. It may be easier to start by looking at the rear, where the **tailpipe** is the obvious end. You'll notice pipes and curved-rectangular or circular cannisters (**muffler** and **resonator**) spliced into the piping as it approaches the front of the car.

At the front, the design of the system varies according to engine. With a V-type engine (V-6 or V-8 or even V-4), the piping will fork, with one branch going to each side of the engine. On an engine in which all the cylinders are in line, the piping will go to one side of the engine.

Near the engine, the piping will connect to the **exhaust manifold**, introduced earlier. The exhaust manifold, which is bolted to the side of the engine, has a branch at each cylinder, to accept the burned exhaust gases and transfer them into the exhaust system.

Before you leave the engine, look around for the engine/oil filter. Its mounting angle will vary from car to car, and it's possible that you also can see it from the top of the engine compartment. In most cases, however, it is more visible, and more accessible for service, from underneath.

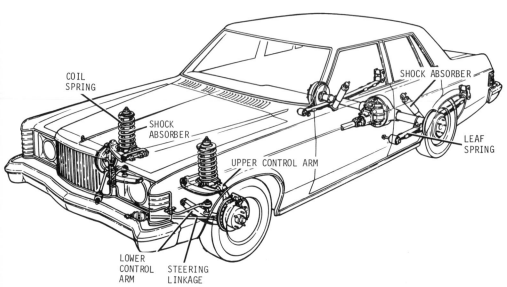

COIL
SPRING

SHOCK ABSORBER

SHOCK
ABSORBER

LEAF
SPRING

UPPER CONTROL ARM

LOWER
CONTROL   STEERING
ARM   LINKAGE

1-11.   Phantom view of car shows front and rear suspension systems. Coil spring, shown on top of upper control arm, may also be positioned between upper and lower arms. Shock absorbers in front are inside the coil spring. The rear suspension contains leaf springs.

SUSPENSION SYSTEM. This system connects the car's chassis to the wheels, and absorbs the bumps as the car travels down the road. At the front of the car, each wheel has its own suspension system, so it can act independently of the other. At the rear of most cars, there is one system, but with individual components at each wheel, as shown in Figs. 1-11 and 1-12.

The key parts of the front suspension are the **control arms**, which are hinged arms that permit the wheel to move up and down when it hits a bump or pothole rather than having the entire car absorb the bump. A coil spring or a twist-spring, called a torsion bar, is used to absorb the shocks. Once the spring action starts, it is difficult to stop, and here the **shock absorber**, really a spring damper, comes into play. It has a fluid-filled cylinder and a piston that work to slow down the spring. Otherwise the car would just continue to rock up and down.

Ball joints are also important parts of the front suspension. They are little swivel joints that connect the control arms to a part called the steering knuckle, to which both the wheel and the steering linkages are connected. As the ball joints operate, they must accept a lot of impacts from the wheel hitting road irregularities. To help extend their life, they have a tiny nipple through which grease can be injected (Fig. 1-13). The nipple, called a grease fitting, may be covered with mud and other road film, so wipe around with a rag until you find it.

The rear suspension's wheels do not steer, so the rear suspension design is much simpler. Each wheel is mounted on a shaft from the rear axle, which is the component that distributes the power to turn the wheels. At each end of the rear axle is a spring and shock absorber. Most cars have either coil or leaf springs, but torsion bars also may be used.

1-12. Underside view of a car shows lower control arms and steering linkage.

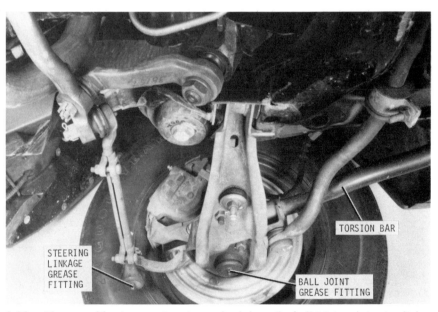

1-13. Close-up of front suspension at one wheel shows the ball-joint and steering-linkage grease fittings.

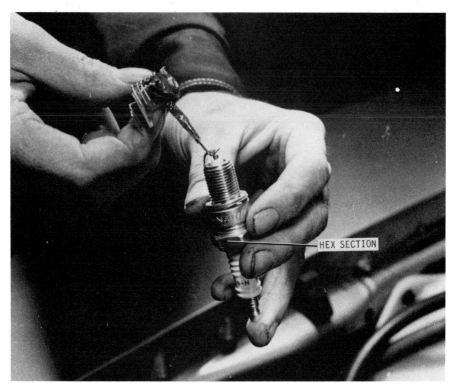

HEX SECTION

1-14. Hexagonal section on the spark plug is the part that accepts the wrench so the plug can be unthreaded or installed.

STEERING SYSTEM. This system starts at the **steering wheel**, which is connected to a long shaft that fits into a box full of gears. The gears turn an arm that projects outside the box and is connected to a system of linkages that resembles that children's toy, the pantograph. The steering linkage has several pivot points (see Fig. 1-13) and at most of them are grease fittings. As with the ball joints, clean off dirt and you'll find them.

The basic tour is over. If you've found all the parts described, you have located everything necessary to do a substantial amount of work on your car. Anything else you must service will either be on one of the major components you have located, or connected to it. Before you prepare to charge into automotive work, take a second look and see how many of the components you must service are attached.

The most common method of attachment is by bolt or screw, possibly also a nut. Hoses and flexible ducts are held by clamps, which also are operated by turning a bolt, nut, or screw, although some may be made of spring wire. Or the part itself may have a threaded section and a hex to accommodate a wrench. The spark plug (Fig. 1-14) is an example of this. Still another method of attachment you may encounter is the snap ring, a C-shaped ring that fits into a groove of a rod. Many linkages, including those at the carburetor, are held together with snap rings.

2 | Tools for Servicing Your Car

You can't service a car with a pair of pliers and a screwdriver any more. In fact, it is doubtful that it ever really could be done. This doesn't mean you will have to make an enormous investment to get started, for the basic equipment is inexpensive and you can add tools as you expand your repertoire.

Many of the basic items you may already have, such as slot and Phillips-head screwdrivers, assorted pliers and perhaps even some wrenches. Here is what you need.

RAISING THE CAR. The most important purchase is equipment with which to raise the car and support it safely, and you have several choices, depending on your budget and what kind of work you plan to do.

Hydraulic jack. The best piece of equipment for raising a car is a hydraulic floor jack (Fig. 2-1). It has wheels or casters, so it rolls easily into position under

2-1. Hydraulic floor jack has wheels or casters for easy positioning, simple pump handle to raise car quickly. Jack has raised car at front crossmember, and safety stands are in place under the A-shaped suspension arms at the wheels.

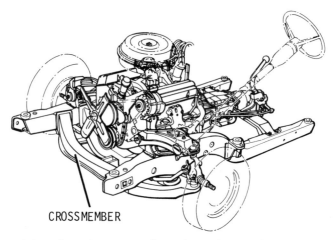

CROSSMEMBER

2-2. Chassis has crossmember at front. This is the best central jacking point. For lifting car at one wheel, jack under the suspension arm.

the front crossmember (Fig. 2-2), which is part of the car's chassis. Just turn the handle clockwise until it locks, then pump the handle. When the car is raised high enough for you to slip underneath, support it with safety stands, which are adjustable supports placed under A-shaped suspension arms at the wheels. See Fig. 2-3 for rear-end jacking.

A suitable hydraulic floor jack has a capacity of at least 3,000 pounds ($1^1/_2$ tons) and a basic weekend mechanic's version, sold in discount houses, is priced from $60 to $100. Adjustable safety stands are $3 each and up. Select stands with a support capacity of at least 3000 pounds each. Once the stands are in position, the jack is lowered and the car rests entirely on the stands.

You cannot use your car's bumper jack to raise the car, for it will not normally lift it high enough to place stands in position underneath. Even if it did, the bumper jack alone isn't safe enough for the moment it takes to slip underneath to position the stands.

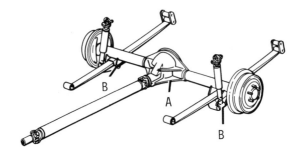

B

A

B

2-3. To raise car at rear, place the jack under the center of the rear axle housing, point A in illustration. Place safety stands at each side of the axle housing, points B.

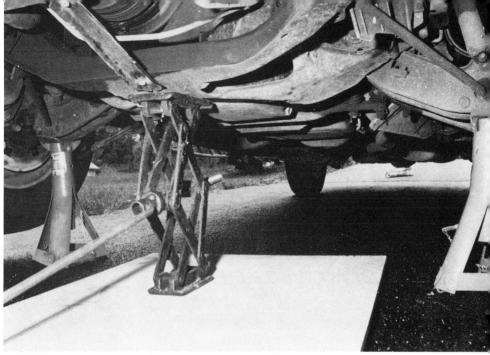

2-4. Scissors jack is an inexpensive way to raise a car. As with a hydraulic jack, safety stands are required.

Scissors jack. A second choice for raising the car is the scissors jack (Fig. 2-4). This jack has a giant screw and a handle that you twist to turn the screw. As the screw is turned, the jack expands in scissors fashion, and once the car is raised sufficiently, the safety stands are positioned and the jack is lowered.

Scissors jacks range in price from $12 for basic models to more than $40 for those with casters or wheels for easy positioning (Fig. 2-5). Scissors jacks require more time and effort to raise the car than the hydraulic jack, but their lower cost recommends them for the person who is not planning to do extensive work.

2-5. This scissors jack is a premium model, with wheels for easy positioning.

2-6. Set of ramps can be made of wood as shown, or purchased ready-made (of steel) from automotive discount houses.

Ramps. The third choice (Fig. 2-6) is a set of ramps (make your own or buy for $18 up). You simply drive the car onto the ramps, apply the emergency brake, and place the transmission lever in Park (on automatics) or first (on manuals). There's a knack to driving up the ramps instead of just pushing them forward when the wheels touch them, but a few tries and you'll learn how to do it.

Wheel chocks. When the front end of the car is raised, the parking brake and the transmission can prevent the car from rolling off the ramps or jack stands. If the rear is raised with a jack, however, there is no restraint for the front wheels. A simple, inexpensive solution is the wheel chock, a metal bracket that is wedged against each front wheel (Fig. 2-7). In its absence, you can use a piece of wood, brick, etc.

2-7. Wheel chock is being placed against the front wheel to prevent the car from rolling forward off the jack when the rear end is raised.

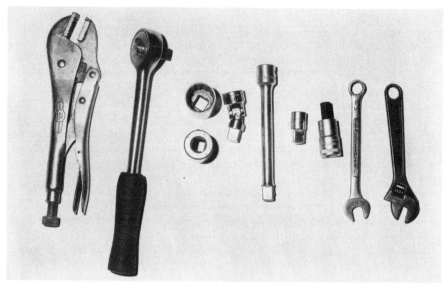

2-8. These are the standard hand tools you should have, in addition to pliers and screwdrivers. From left to right: vise pliers, ratchet, two sockets (notice square hole in socket to accept ratchet square), universal joint, medium-size extension, very short extension, Allen wrench bit that fits into ratchet, combination open-end and box wrench (box section at top; open-end at bottom), and adjustable open-end wrench.

RATCHET AND SOCKET. Of all the hand tools used in auto mechanics, the ratchet and socket are the most useful (Fig. 2-8). The socket is a cylindrical wrench that is internally shaped to fit the hexagonal head of a nut or bolt. The top of the socket has a square hole (3/8 or 1/2 inch in customary automotive usage) into which the ratchet fits.

The ratchet is a handle that is designed to move freely in one direction and lock in the other. It has a knob that permits setting it for clockwise or counterclockwise lock (Fig. 2-9).

2-9. Knob on ratchet head permits setting it to lock clockwise or counterclockwise.

A square protrusion on the ratchet fits into the square hole in the socket, permitting the ratchet and socket to work as a single assembly. If set to lock in the counterclockwise direction, the handle can pull on the socket and force-loosen a nut or bolt (or anything with a hexagonal surface). If set to lock in the clockwise direction, the ratchet will pull on the socket to tighten the nut or bolt.

The socket is small, so it can fit into tight quarters. Often the ratchet cannot. For that reason, an extension rod and universal joint are often used.

The extension rod has a square protrusion on one end (just like the one on the ratchet) so it can fit into the socket, and a hole on the other end (just like the socket) so it can fit into the protrusion from the ratchet. Extensions come in various lengths and they can be fitted into each other, to form even longer extensions.

The universal joint is a swivel joint that permits the ratchet to be operated at an angle to the socket, for use in tight quarters. Depending on the access angle, the universal joint can be fitted directly into the socket, between two extension rods, or between an extension rod and the ratchet.

Also available are ratchets with a universal joint built in, and sockets with a universal joint attached, for working in unusually tight quarters (Fig. 2-10).

The typical weekend mechanic will find the following the most useful:
• A ratchet with a 3/8-inch square (called a 3/8-inch drive)
• An assortment of sockets, 3/8-inch-drive. The business end of the socket, which fits onto the hex nut or bolt, should be in the following American sizes: 3/8, 7/16, 1/2, 9/16, 5/8, 11/16, and 3/4 inch. If you have a car with metric fittings, the most useful metric sizes are: 8, 9, 10, 11, 12, 13, 14, 15, 17, and 19 millimeters (mm).

You also will need a spark plug socket, which is deeper than the standard socket, to fit over the length of the plug. There are two common sizes, 13/16 and 5/8 inch.

A single universal joint in the 3/8-inch-drive size and several short extension rods (from 2 to 6 or 8 inches long) will complete your needs.

Prices of sets of sockets, ratchet and extension rods range from $15 up, and universal joints are about $3 to $5. Check the automotive departments of discount stores for sales.

OPEN-END AND BOX WRENCHES. The open-end and box wrenches also are indispensable additions to the toolbox. The open-end is a wrench with a C-shaped end that fits snugly around four of the six sides of the hexagonal nut or bolt. The end is offset slightly so it can be flipped over and placed over the nut or bolt at a different angle. This permits it to be used in tight quarters where another type of wrench would not fit.

The box wrench fits over all six sides of the nut or bolt, providing a more secure grip. The circular wall of the wrench end is made as thin as possible so it can fit into relatively tight places. Generally, the better the steel, the thinner the wall can be made.

Box and open-end wrenches are often combined, with a box on one end of the handle and an open-end on the other. Or there may be two box or open-end sizes on each wrench (see Fig. 2-8).

The same sizes that are most useful in sockets also are recommended for box and open-end wrenches, plus 1/4 and 5/16 inch in American sizes and 6mm in metric.

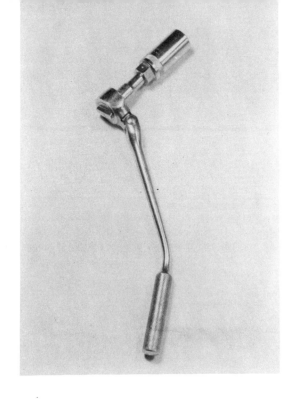

2-10. This ratchet has a curved handle and universal joint in head, and is made primarily for removing spark plugs from areas with limited access.

As with socket wrenches, box and open ends are combined into sets, and the best prices are during a sale at the automotive departments of discount stores. A good wrench will look good. Its surfaces will be nicely machined and it will be obviously sturdy. Prices vary substantially, from $10 and up.

SCREWDRIVERS. A good screwdriver should cost $1.50 or more. It will be made of chrome vanadium steel and have fine vertical milling marks on the tip.

It is almost impossible to specify the sizes of slot and Phillips-head screwdrivers you will find most useful on your car. About all you can do is buy a variety and find out what fits the screws you will be trying to loosen. There are three aspects to screwdriver size: width of the tip, length of the shank, and size of the handle. Long-shank screwdrivers with big handles permit you to reach recessed screws and apply a lot of twisting force. However, they won't fit into a lot of places, in which case the short screwdriver with the big handle—called a stub handle screwdriver—is an essential tool.

The thickness of the tip determines whether or not you will fit the screwdriver into the slot. On the simple single-slot screw, it is generally easy to tell, but sometimes you can force the too-wide tip partly into the slot and ruin it when you try to turn.

The Phillips-head screwdriver, which goes into a cross-slot, poses a similar problem. If you force it into a too-small slot, it won't fit in all the way and the slot will be damaged. The same thing happens if the screwdriver is too small for the slot. The screwdriver doesn't grip properly and damages the slot.

Sounds like a lot to worry about, but if you have a small assortment, you'll have one that's a good fit for the typical automotive slot. Generally, a small, medium, and large in both single-slot and Phillips designs will cover all your needs.

19

PLIERS. Everyone has a pair of slip-joint pliers and most homeowners have a couple of vise-type locking pliers. In automotive service, however, a mechanic may have dozens of specialty pliers. The most useful in basic automotive work are:

Needle-nose pliers. Just what the name says, they have long tapered jaws to reach into tight quarters.

Wire-stripping pliers. They will remove the insulation from the end of a strip of wire and also will crimp on wire terminals. A beginner can generally put off a purchase of this type.

Spring clamp pliers. These are designed to fit the spring clamps commonly used for many hose connections on cars. If your car doesn't have several of these clamps (**Fig. 2-11**), don't make the investment. A single clamp or two, in an acces-

2-11.   Spring-clamp pliers are useful only if your car has lots of spring clamps.

sible location, can be removed with slip-joint or vise pliers (it's a bit of a struggle, but it can be done) and you can replace the spring clamp type with a 25-cent clamp that doesn't require the tool, which is about $4.

There are other tools required for basic automotive service, such as a wrench for removing an oil filter, a grease gun, etc. The details on these tools are covered in the chapters that explain the service procedures.

3 | Servicing the Cooling System

The cooling system of your engine is probably no real stranger to you. Nearly four out of five car owners install their own antifreeze and that's a basic cooling-system service.

The cooling system does exactly what the name says; it takes away heat from the engine and expels it into the atmosphere. Without a properly functioning system, the heat built up from the burning gases would soon overheat the engine.

The cooling system (Fig. 3-1) is filled with a mixture of antifreeze and water. The mixture flows through passages cast into the engine, where it absorbs heat. A water pump, mounted at the front of the engine and driven by a belt-and-pulley arrangement from the crankshaft, circulates the mixture, called coolant, through the engine, then out through a hose into the radiator.

A fan on the front of the engine (generally mounted on the water pump pulley so it is spun by the drive belt) draws air in, between the radiator tubes. Fins help direct the air around the tubes, to absorb heat from the coolant. After the coolant

3-1. Typical cooling system on a water-cooled car. Belt-driven water pump circulates water-antifreeze mixture between engine, radiator, and heater.

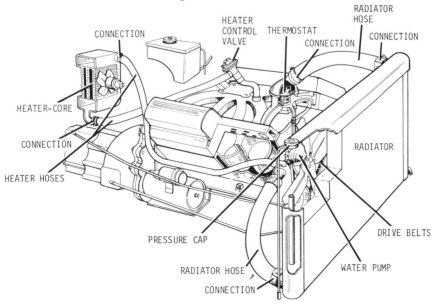

flows through the radiator and gives up its heat, it is drawn back into the engine by the water pump, through a second hose at the bottom of the radiator.

THERMOSTAT. Although the engine must be cooled, it cannot be cooled too much. Engine parts work better at a certain temperature. You surely have observed that the engine performs best when it's "warmed up." To warm up the engine quickly and maintain the temperature at a desired level, a thermostat is used. The thermostat is an automatic temperature-sensitive valve that is closed until the coolant warms up. The closed thermostat keeps the coolant circulating only through the engine, instead of allowing it to cool in the radiator. As the engine warms up, the thermostat opens and permits the coolant to flow through it, into the hose to the top of the radiator.

The coolant in a typical engine is maintained at 180 to 205 degrees F. by the opening and closing of the thermostat. On a hot day, however, coolant temperature may rise to nearly 250 degrees F., particularly if the engine is working hard (such as when the car is climbing a mountain) or is sitting in heavy traffic, where air circulation is poor.

Water boils at 212 degrees F. and even a 50-50 mixture of water and antifreeze boils at about 225 degrees F. To prevent the coolant from boiling away, it is placed under pressure. Each pound-per-square-inch that the coolant is pressurized adds between 2 and 3 degrees to the boiling point, and the typical cooling system operates with 14 pounds per square inch. This raises the boiling point of a 50-50 mixture from 225 to almost 265 degrees F.

The pressure is not applied. It is allowed to build up. As the coolant absorbs heat, it tries to expand but because it's in a confined space (engine passages, hoses, and radiator), it builds up pressure. This buildup of pressure raises the boiling point so the coolant does not boil away.

There is a limit to how much pressure the system can stand without bursting at the radiator seams or elsewhere, and to keep the pressure within limits, a pressure cap is used.

The cap is located on top of the radiator; it is the part you twist off to add water or antifreeze to the system. The cap has a spring-loaded valve (Fig. 3-2) that

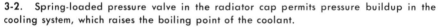

3-2. Spring-loaded pressure valve in the radiator cap permits pressure buildup in the cooling system, which raises the boiling point of the coolant.

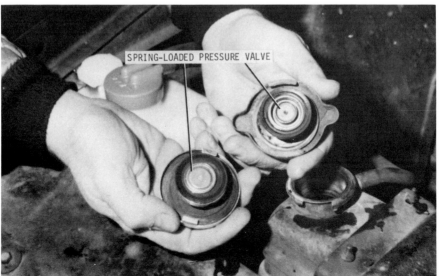

bears against the radiator fill neck, to prevent the coolant from expanding and forcing its way out of the system. When pressure reaches the designed level, usually 14 pounds per square inch, the pressurized coolant can push up on the spring and force open the valve, allowing coolant to escape and reduce pressure.

On older cars, the coolant just flowed out a tube to the ground. On most newer cars, the coolant flows into a reservoir. When the engine is allowed to cool down, the coolant contracts and a second valve in the cap opens, allowing the "lost" coolant to be drawn back, from the reservoir into the radiator. The radiator is always topped up automatically.

HEATER. The cooling system also serves a second function, to warm the passenger compartment in cold weather. A tubular finned part called the heater core, somewhat like a miniature radiator, is placed in a duct at the passenger compartment (Fig. 3-1) and some of the coolant is circulated through it, by hoses connected to the engine and water pump. The hose connected to the top of the engine is the inlet—coolant flows from the engine through it into the heater core. It flows through the heater core into the outlet hose, which takes it to the water pump for circulation through the engine.

An electric fan, called the blower, is turned on when you flip a dashboard switch, and it blows air through the heater core, much like the fan at the radiator. The warmed air continues to flow through the ductwork into the passenger compartment.

With this basic understanding of cooling system operation, you can proceed to service many of the components.

HOSES. Radiator and heater hoses are subjected to a great deal of heat, both from the engine and the hot coolant they transfer. The coolant also gradually eats away at the inside of the hoses. In time, the hoses fail.

Hoses are inexpensive, and they're not difficult to replace if you can do the job in the convenience of your driveway. Therefore, it's a good idea to check them periodically and replace them if necessary.

Feel the hoses. If they are heat-hardened, or if they feel very spongy, they're near the end of their useful life. A good hose should feel flexible but not spongy, firm but not hard. When you're in an auto supply store, feel the new merchandise so you'll know.

Selecting replacements. You've got to buy the right parts before you can install them. If possible, take the specific car with you when you go to buy hoses, so you can match them up. As a beginner, your best bet is to buy in an auto parts store that also serves professional mechanics. The countermen generally are more knowledgeable than the sales people in the automotive departments of discount houses.

In general, an upper radiator hose is the simplest purchase. This hose normally follows a straight path from the top of the engine to the top of the radiator, and so it is usually a straight hose, corrugated so it can be curved during installation.

The lower radiator hose takes a different path on every engine. Therefore it is likely to be a molded type. There's no margin for error with a molded hose, particularly if it has more than one connection point. Some have an additional small hose, called a bypass, built in.

Heater hoses are sold by length and inside diameter; however, it is usually unnecessary to measure your hose, as the proper size for your car will be listed in a catalog at the supply store.

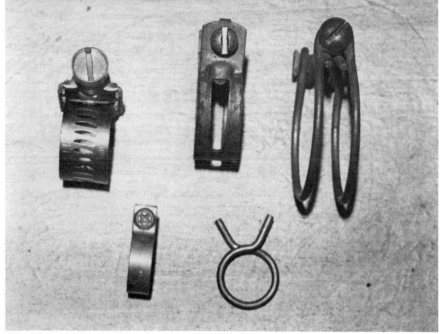

3-3. Hose clamps in common use (top row, left to right): worm-drive, double-band, double-wire. Bottom left is single-band design, right is spring-clamp type.

Hose clamps. Hose clamps should also be purchased with care. The clamp used by the car manufacturer may be the spring type (Fig. 3-3), which is reusable but is a poor design that digs into a hose. Also, it can't be tightened, so if it loses tension you must remove and discard it. Or the original clamp may be a cheap band type that corrodes and often must be broken to remove. The best clamp is the worm-drive type (Fig. 3-4). It is easily tightened or loosened with a screwdriver or wrench, and it can be opened all the way and installed even with the hose already in place. These clamps come in sizes to fit different hoses.

New hose clamps are not mandatory for hose replacement. If there's any question about struggling with an original clamp, however, just get it off any way you can, even if you have to pry it apart with a screwdriver and cut it open with tin snips. A new worm-drive clamp is so inexpensive that it hardly pays to use any other kind.

3-4. Worm-drive clamp can be loosened or tightened with a screwdriver in the slot, or with a wrench on the hex as shown.

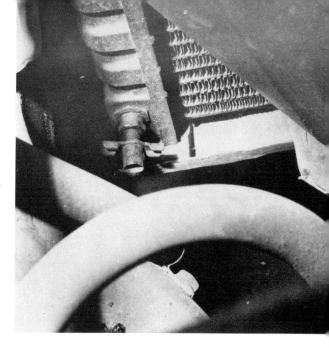

3-5. Cock in the bottom of the radiator is the most common drain in use.

Removing the old hose. If you are merely removing a hose in the course of doing other work, you must get it off without damaging it. Hoses have a tendency to heat-seal to the necks on which they fit, and if you aren't careful you can damage a usable hose.

If the antifreeze is less than a year old and therefore reusable, begin by draining the coolant into a clean pan. Draining will minimize spillage during hose replacement.

To drain the radiator, open the drain cock (Fig. 3-5) or remove the plug with a wrench (Fig. 3-6). Some cars have neither a drain cock nor plug, primarily 1972–73 General Motors cars, the Volkswagen Rabbit, Dasher, and Scirocco, and the Audi Fox. On these cars you must disconnect the lower hose from the radiator.

3-6. Some radiators have a plug in the bottom, removable with a wrench. Type shown can be removed with box or open-end; some plugs are recessed and can only be removed with a socket wrench and ratchet.

25

3-7. Rough rubber helps to get a grip on a round radiator cap.

Next, remove the radiator cap. If the cooling system has a reservoir, the cap is completely round and not easy to hold. Use a piece of rough rubber (Fig. 3-7) or a radiator cap removing wrench. Press down on the cap, to compress the spring inside, and twist until the cap is free. If the cap has a lever built into the top, lift it and twist (Fig. 3-8). Removing the cap permits air to enter the radiator so it drains completely.

Now loosen the hose clamp and move it off the section that fits on the neck. Now try to turn the hose section at the neck. If it turns, grasp the hose just past the edge of the neck and try to pull as you turn it back and forth. If the hose doesn't come off, insert a thin-bladed screwdriver between hose and neck and gently work it in, all around, to break the seal (Fig. 3-9). Be careful not to pry with the screwdriver; you can damage the inner surface of the hose or even the neck. Once the screwdriver has been worked in all around, you should be able to turn and pull off the hose.

3-8. If radiator cap has a lever, pull up before trying to remove the cap.

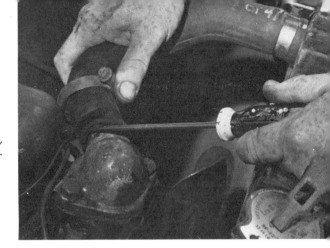

3-9. If a radiator hose sticks, gently pry it off with a thin screwdriver.

However, if the hose is going to be replaced, just cut it off the neck with a razor blade. Cut the hose at or near the neck, then slice the remaining section along its length and peel it off the neck.

Heater hoses may be an exception to the don't-cut-unless-you're-replacing rule. Many heater hoses have enough slack so you can cut the hose at the end of the neck and still have enough left to reinstall it without stretching.

You may also find that the heater hose is defective only on the section that is close to the engine. If both ends of the hose are accessible, the simplest procedure is to replace the entire hose. On many cars, however, the heater hose connections at the heater are not easily accessible—you may not even be able to see them without looking under the dashboard. Then you must cut off only the defective (usually heat-hardened) section near the engine and join the good remaining hose to a section of new hose, using a part called a flushing tee. This tee (Fig. 3-10) is designed to make flushing the cooling system easier and its use

3-10. Flushing tee can be used as a connector between sections of heater hose. Secure with clamps, then thread sealing cap onto the top of the tee to complete job.

is described later in this chapter. However, it also can be used as a connector for two sections of heater hose.

The tee is normally installed in the heater inlet hose when used for flushing cooling systems, but it can also be installed in the outlet hose as a simple connector. There are other types of connectors, but the tee is both inexpensive and readily available. *Note*: If you are putting it into the heater outlet hose solely as a connector, don't buy a complete flushing tee kit. A tee and a couple of retaining clamps are all you need and these are available as individual parts in many auto parts stores.

Installing the new hose. Whether installing a new hose or refitting the old one, begin by cleaning off the hose neck with a wire brush. If you have trouble pushing the new hose onto the neck, first coat the neck with soap solution as a lubricant. Place the clamp on the hose and push the hose as far onto the neck as it can go. Position the clamp at least 1/4 inch from the end of the neck, preferably halfway between the end of the neck and the end of the hose, and tighten it securely.

FLUSHING THE COOLING SYSTEM. Antifreeze not only keeps water from freezing in winter, but raises the boiling point in summer. It also contains chemicals called inhibitors that prevent buildup of rust and corrosion in the cooling system.

A 50-50 water and antifreeze mixture is considered a minimum, with 70 percent antifreeze an ideal figure. With this much antifreeze, the freezing point is dropped to minus 70 degrees F., more than you really need, but the boiling point is raised to 238 degrees F., and with 14 pounds per square inch of pressure, to nearly 275 degrees. This gives you a reasonable margin of safety, for even a healthy cooling system leaks some coolant, and if you top up with water, you reduce the antifreeze concentration.

Most people who add their own antifreeze just open the radiator drain cock or remove the plug, allow the coolant inside to drain out, then refill the radiator with antifreeze. This is the extent of their cooling system maintenance.

The radiator, however, only holds 25 to 45 per cent of the coolant. The rest is in the engine, the hoses and the heater core. Most of the coolant, therefore, and any rust particles it contains, remain in the system. What you should do is flush the system out completely. It's not a difficult job.

Tool requirements. The only tools necessary to flush out a cooling system are:
• a pair of pliers to open the drain cock or a socket and ratchet to remove the drain plug;
• a screwdriver or spring clamp pliers (Fig. 3-11), so you can disconnect hoses;
• a stopper plug big enough to plug the neck onto which the heater outlet hose fits (tapered to about 3/4-inch diameter);
• a garden hose;
• an old radiator hose of the same diameter as the one at the top of your radiator. This is not essential, but if you change a radiator hose, keep the old hose for flushing work.

Inspecting the coolant. Remove the radiator cap and look at the coolant. If you can't see inside the radiator, draw out a coolant sample with a syringe, empty it into a glass and inspect it. If it's rusty colored or filled with rust particles, pour a

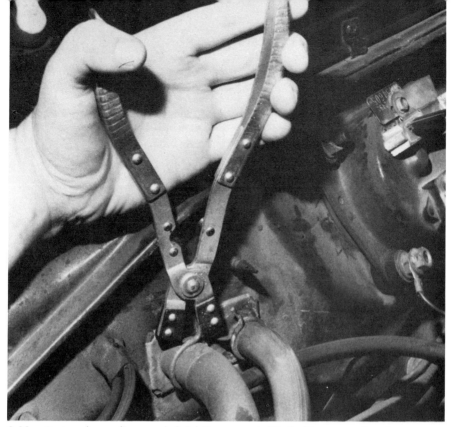

3-11.   Spring clamp pliers are helpful if your car is fitted with many spring clamps.

container of cooling system cleaner into the radiator. The cleaner, called "fast flush," will work while you drive (about 100 miles).

Reinstall the radiator cap, press down and twist until it locks in place. Drive the car the specified number of miles, with the heater on, so the core also will be cleaned, then drain the radiator (see Fig. 3-12).

Flushing. Determine the capacity of your car's cooling system. This information may be in your owner's manual or can be obtained from a reference manual you can inspect at most automotive parts stores. Buy enough antifreeze to equal 70 per cent of the total capacity, including heater. Disconnect the smaller diameter hose (the heater outlet hose) from its neck on the water pump. Force the stopper plug into the hose neck. It should fit tightly but project enough so you can pull it out with a pair of ordinary pliers when the job is done.

Disconnect the upper radiator hose at the engine, then loosen the hose clamp at the radiator end. Twist the hose at the radiator so it doesn't aim near the fan. Coolant will be flowing from this hose later on, and if it hits the fan you'll be splattered. If you have the old radiator hose, force it into the disconnected end; you'll now have an effectively longer hose you can more easily aim away from the engine.

Force the garden hose into the end of the disconnected heater hose (Fig. 3-12), then turn the heater controls on to maximum. Start the engine, let it idle and immediately open the household water valve (the bibcock) to the gardern hose.

3-12.

FLUSHING A COOLING SYSTEM
(first stage)

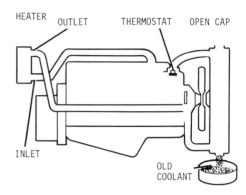

Drain the radiator.

Disconnect the heater outlet hose, cork the neck, and attach a garden hose.

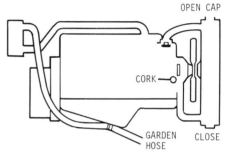

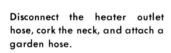

Disconnect the upper radiator hose from the engine.

Water will flow from the garden hose into the heater outlet hose, backwards through the heater core into the heater inlet hose, into the engine, through the lower radiator hose, up or across the radiator and out the upper hose (see Fig. 3-13).

When the water running out of the upper hose is absolutely clean for a two-minute period, stop the engine and turn off the water to the garden hose. Reconnect the upper radiator hose to the engine, but leave the heater outlet hose disconnected and the stopper plug in place. Drain the radiator once more, then close the cock or replace the plug.

Pour antifreeze into the radiator fill neck, and when the radiator is nearly full, turn the heater controls to high and start the engine. The antifreeze in the radia-

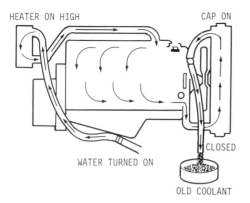

HEATER ON HIGH

CAP ON

CLOSED

WATER TURNED ON

OLD COOLANT

Turn heater to maximum, start engine, and turn on water.

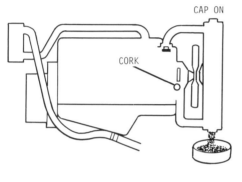

CAP ON

CORK

When coolant runs clean, stop flushing and drain radiator.

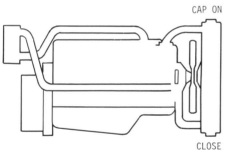

CAP ON

CLOSE

Close radiator drain, add antifreeze, and reconnect hoses.

tor will be drawn into the engine, and the pure water in the system will be forced out of the heater outlet hose (which was left disconnected). Keep pouring the antifreeze into the radiator until the full amount is installed, then quickly stop the engine, pull the stopper plug from the water pump and reconnect the heater hose. It is possible for a small amount of antifreeze to mix with the water and escape through the heater hose before you have emptied the containers into the radiator. The amount, however, will be insignificant.

Flushing with a tee. There is a second simple method for flushing a cooling system, using a flushing tee kit, which is an inexpensive item available in most auto parts stores and the automotive departments of many discount houses. The

31

3-14. Tee secured in heater hose with clamps. Add cap and installation is permanent.

tee itself was introduced to you earlier in this chapter as a connector for two heater hose sections, but its primary purpose is to permit flushing the cooling system without disconnecting any hoses.

The kit includes the tee (Fig 3-14), which is spliced into the heater inlet hose (the one that doesn't go to the water pump), an adapter that mates a garden hose to the threaded crossbar of the tee, and a cap that threads onto and seals the crossbar opening when the flushing is complete. This permits the tee to be permanently installed without interfering with the normal operation of the cooling sys-

3-15. Deflector in radiator cap neck is aimed forward to prevent water from splashing on engine.

3-16. Special adapter permits connecting garden hose to flushing tee.

tem. The kit also includes an L-shaped water deflector that fits into the radiator fill neck, eliminating the need to disconnect the upper radiator hose.

To flush out the system with a tee, remove the radiator cap and force the deflector into the fill neck. Aim the outlet nozzle forward so water doesn't splash onto the engine (Fig. 3-15).

Remove the cap from the tee crossbar and connect the adapter tightly (Fig. 3-16) and then connect the garden hose to the other half of the adapter.

Start the engine, let it idle, and turn the heater controls to high. Turn on the water to the garden hose. The water will flow through the heater hose into the heater, then from heater outlet hose into the water pump, out the lower radiator hose into the radiator, up or across the radiator and out the fill neck through the deflector nozzle. The water also will flow from the heater inlet hose into the engine itself, where it will circulate and force dirty coolant into the lower radiator hose and then into the radiator.

When the water coming out of the deflector runs clean for two minutes, stop the engine, turn off the water to the hose, remove the deflector and disconnect the garden hose. Unthread the adapter from the tee crossbar.

To install antifreeze, drain the radiator (then close the cock or replace the plug) and pour the antifreeze in through the fill neck. The antifreeze will force water out of the open flushing tee. If you wish to speed up the flow of water from the tee, start the engine and turn the heater controls to maximum. When you have installed all the antifreeze, stop the engine and thread the cap onto the tee, as hand tight as you can make it.

RADIATOR CAP. As explained at the beginning of this chapter, the radiator cap is more than a simple cover on the radiator fill neck. It has important jobs to do and if it fails, the engine will overheat.

Remove the cap and inspect it.

• On cars with an overflow reservoir, look at and feel the gasket on the inner circumference (Fig. 3-17). If this gasket is torn or has deep indentations, and the radiator is low on coolant, the gasket is not sealing. If so, it is permitting the cooling system to draw in air instead of coolant from the reservoir, defeating the purpose of the reservoir. Replace the cap.

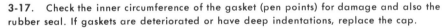

3-17. Check the inner circumference of the gasket (pen points) for damage and also the rubber seal. If gaskets are deteriorated or have deep indentations, replace the cap.

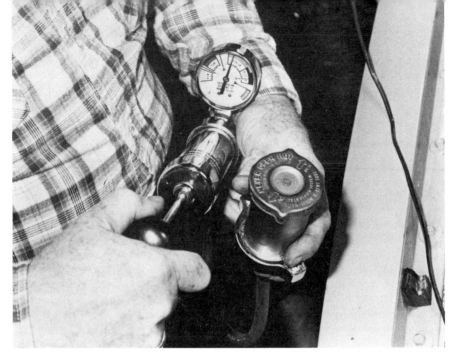

3-18. Professional mechanic has a pressure gauge to check the cap against factory specifications. The cap should hold pressure as shown.

• On all caps, inspect the pressure-valve rubber seal (Fig. 3-17). If the rubber seal is deteriorated or has deep indentations, it won't seal properly and coolant will leak out. Even if the coolant goes into an overflow reservoir the engine will overheat. Most service stations have a special pressure tester to check the cap (Fig. 3-18) and to determine if the seal is leaking or not. Normally, the pressure-valve seal is suspect if the engine overheats within five to ten miles.

• Check the vacuum valve (Fig. 3-19). Slip a fingernail under this valve, pull it down and see if it springs back. *Note:* On some cars the valve is weighted and should be open if the cap is held vertical. This valve is used on all systems to admit coolant from the reservoir or, on systems without a reservoir, to purge the undesirable vacuum with fresh air from outside. If the valve is stuck in closed position, replace the cap.

3-19. The cap also has a vacuum valve that usually is spring loaded. Get a fingernail underneath and pull down. It should not stick and should spring back.

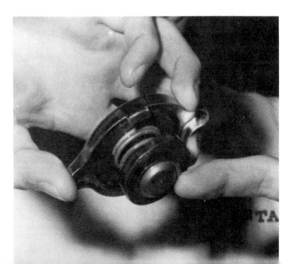

4 | Lubrication

Without oil, the moving parts in your engine soon would seize from friction or wear out. The oil never wears out, but it becomes contaminated with particles from burned gases and abrasive dirt in the air. It also becomes diluted with unburned fuel droplets that slip past the pistons. Finally, high engine temperatures and burned exhaust gases that also slip past the pistons turn oil into a thick mixture called sludge, which is anything but an ideal lubricant.

The engine's oil filter removes many dirt particles and much of the sludge, but in time it clogs. To insure a flow of clean engine oil to all the moving parts, the oil and filter should be changed at least twice a year, four times a year if you live in areas with very high summer and very low winter temperatures and poor air quality, and you do a great deal of short-trip driving.

BUYING PARTS AND TOOLS. Changing oil and filter is a basic job that nearly 40 percent of American motorists do themselves. You will need:

• A method of safely supporting the car so you can slip underneath. Pick one of the methods described in Chapter 2. *Note*: On some cars there is enough clearance under the engine so you can change oil and filter without jacking up the car. Check before you invest.

• A wrench to remove the oil drain plug (Fig. 4-1).

• A flat pan of at least six-quart capacity to catch the oil drained from the engine. A plastic household pan is suitable.

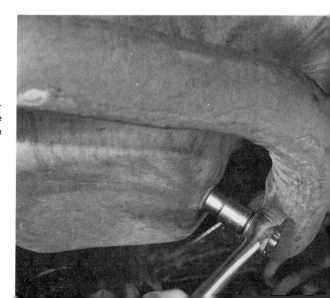

4-1. Wrench is needed to remove oil drain plug. If you have a socket set, you should have a socket that fits it.

4-2. Band-type filter wrench is commonly used to remove filter.

• A filter wrench, a band-type wrench (Fig. 4-2) that makes filter removal very easy. Discount houses sell them for under $1. Or for under $5 you can obtain a combination wrench that will remove the oil drain plug from the engine and the oil filter (Fig. 4-3).

Engine oil. The typical American car requires five quarts of engine oil when the filter (which also holds some oil) also is changed. Although most car manufacturers say that the filter need only be changed at every other oil drain, the filter holds up to a quart of oil. Replacing the filter at the same time as the oil gives the engine a completely fresh charge of oil and, because the filter also is clean, insures the job will last longer.

4-3. A convenient tool is the combination oil filter wrench and oil drain plug wrench, with box-type hex openings for all popular drain plug sizes.

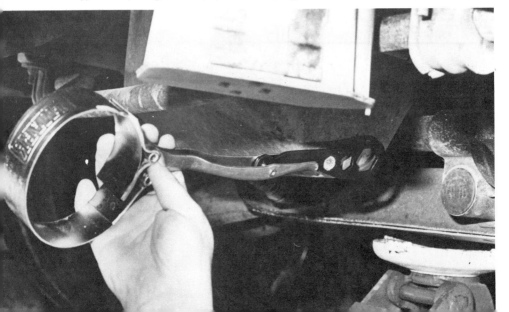

The oil you select should be a name brand of the multi-grade type, such as 10W-30, 10W-40 or 10W-50. The numbers refer to the thickness of the oil at certain temperatures; the lower the number, the thinner the oil. The first part of the number, 10W, is the thickness at zero degrees; the second part, the 30, 40 or 50, is the thickness at 210 degrees.

A 10W-40 oil, for example, has the relative lightness of a 10 oil at low temperature, so it flows freely for good cold-engine lubrication. Oil normally thins out at high temperature, but the multi-grade oil has such great resistance to this that at 210 degrees, it has the thickness of a 40 weight oil, for good high-temperature lubrication. Because multi-grade oils have these dual characteristics, they also are referred to as year-round lubricants.

You should also check the oil can for the service rating. You should see a phrase, "for API service," followed by several two-letter codes. If one of the codes is "SE" the oil is the type recommended for a late-model engine (see Fig. 4-4).

Note: Synthetic oils have recently come onto the market, and despite their high initial price ($4 to $5 a quart), they can be an excellent buy for a number of reasons. First, they can go for a long time without the need for change. The official recommendations, for various legal reasons, are to follow the car maker's oil drain specifications. However, these oils have been tested successfully without change for as much as 50,000 miles, and some oil company engineers admit that even a conservative drain interval would be once every two years. The oil filter, however, should be changed at least once a year, which will require adding some make-up oil. Whenever you add make-up oil, you must use the same brand of synthetic. Another advantage of a quality synthetic: reduced engine friction means better gas mileage (up to 5 percent) and easier starting in winter.

Filter and wrench. Pick a filter according to brand, sticking with the brands you see in service stations and garages. Other brands, including some "house" brands sold in discount houses, are also made by the leading filter manufac-

4-4. Look at the markings on an oil can. The can shown has a lot of letters and numbers, but the ones you are interested in are API Services, SE, and the viscosity, 10W and 40.

turers, but they are often not of the same filtering efficiency. These house brands are not bad filters; it's just that they're not as good as the manufacturer's first line, which carries his brand name.

If you buy in a discount house, read the catalog listings carefully to make sure you're getting the filter for your make, model, year, and engine. If you can't decide between two part numbers, buy both and return the one that doesn't fit.

Next, buy a filter wrench that is the right size for the filter. The wrench's band should close tightly around the filter cannister when you pull the handle (Fig. 4-2). The combination drain plug-filter wrench will fit the filters on American cars and some imports. If the filter is an off-size, look for a filter wrench that is adjustable to cover a wide range of sizes. It costs $3 to $4.

Drain plug wrench. If you buy the combination drain plug-filter wrench, you will have a wrench with all the popular drain plug sizes. But if you want a drain plug wrench, you have to measure the drain plug. Raise and support the front end of the car, slip underneath and look for the drain plug. It will appear to be a bolt threaded into the middle of the sheet-metal oil pan at the bottom of the engine. If you don't already have a wrench that fits it, place a piece of paper over the hexagonal head and with your fingers press down on the paper to form the outline of the hex (see Fig. 4-5). Remove the paper and with a ruler measure the hex as shown in Fig. 4-5 to determine the size wrench you need.

CHANGING THE OIL. The engine should be warm so the oil will be sufficiently thinned to drain completely. Jack up the car and install safety stands, or drive the car onto ramps. Slip underneath with the proper wrench for the drain plug and a household pan to catch the oil. Exert a counterclockwise pull to loosen the plug.

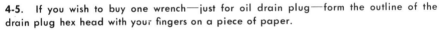

4-5. If you wish to buy one wrench—just for oil drain plug—form the outline of the drain plug hex head with your fingers on a piece of paper.

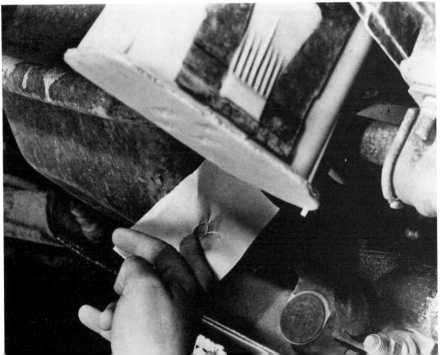

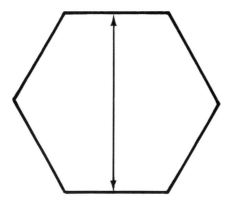

4-6. Measure across the flats of the hex head outline to get the wrench size.

Caution: It's easy to confuse clockwise and counterclockwise directions when lying underneath the car, and you may actually tighten the plug instead of loosening it. If you are unsure, try this: thread a bolt into a nut and take it underneath with you. Hold the nut and bolt with the nut upward and turn the bolt to unthread it from the nut. The direction you turn the bolt is the same that you should turn the drain plug. Or hold a wrist watch up at the drain plug, with 12 o'clock just over the hex.

As soon as the plug is loosened, complete the unthreading by hand, with the household pan underneath the drain. When you get to the last few threads, apply finger pressure to hold the plug in the hole as you unthread it. When the plug is completely loose, held in place only by your fingers, quickly pull it away. This will prevent splashing oil on your arm.

Allow several minutes for the oil to drain out completely. Thread the plug in by hand, then tighten moderately with the wrench. *Note*: Do not force the plug with the wrench. If you have to use force, you are probably cross-threading, and the threads on both the plug and the oil pan will be damaged. The plug will not tighten properly, and even if it feels tight, it probably will loosen and soon leak oil.

If you aren't sure, take out the plug and look at the threads carefully. If they are not damaged, clean them off with a small brush, such as the type from an electric razor. If they are damaged, don't panic and don't try to reuse the plug. The problem is not uncommon and auto parts stores carry kits to solve this problem, all under $5. Instructions provided with the kits will explain how to install them.

Oil filter. Look at your new oil filter and find a similar cannister threaded somewhere onto the engine block. It may be mounted horizontally, vertically, or at an angle. Every one is located differently, so there are no hard-and-fast rules for removal. You may be able to get it off working from the top of the engine compartment or from underneath. Regardless of placement, you will be able to loosen the filter with the filter wrench.

The object is to place the wrench on the filter so that the band tightens up as you pull on the handle in the counterclockwise direction. To do this, note the way the handle must be turned to get the band to close, then place the tool on the filter so the band is closing as you pull the handle counterclockwise. If you put it on wrong, the band will close only when you turn the handle clockwise and you will tighten the filter.

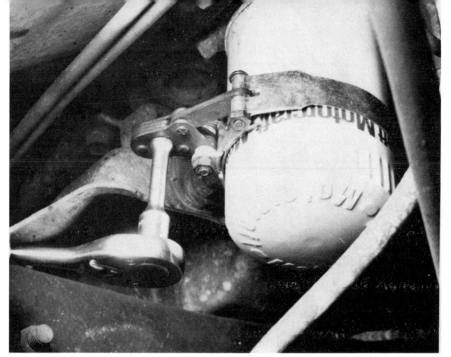

4-8. Oil filter wrench shown also is a band type, but it accepts an extension and ratchet, so it can be used in tight places that an ordinary band wrench cannot.

As you pull the handle to tighten the band, it will probably be necessary to turn the entire wrench slightly so that when the band is completely tight there is some room to swing the handle counterclockwise. If there is no way to do this, perhaps moving the band along the cannister, closer to or farther away from the engine, will put the handle in a good working position.

If the wrench will not work in any position, return it and obtain the type shown in Fig. 4-8. This is similar to the other in that it has a band, but instead of a handle it has a tiny square into which an extension rod fits, permitting it to be turned with a ratchet wrench somewhat removed from the area of the engine.

Once the filter is loose, move the household pan underneath, take off the wrench and complete filter removal by hand. Depending on the filter's mounting angle, some oil in the filter may spill out into the pan.

Installing a new filter. Coat the gasket of the new filter with clean engine oil; then thread the filter onto the engine flange and hand-tighten it. To get a good grip your hands and the filter cannister should be free of oil. Do not try to tighten the filter with the wrench or you surely will overtighten it. The gasket will heat-seal to the engine in normal operation anyway, and you'll have a nearly impossible time trying to remove the filter thousands of miles later.

Engine oil. Now pour the fresh oil into the engine. You can open the can with a can opener and pour through a funnel, or you can obtain a puncturing spout, which does both jobs and makes it easier to pour oil in without spillage (Fig. 4-9).

Where to pour in the oil may not be at all obvious to you if you have never done it before or watched a service station attendant. Most cars have either a thread-on cap on one of the sheet-metal top covers (Fig. 4-10) or a twist-and-pull-off cap on a pipe. Don't pour unless you're sure.

4-9. Puncture spout makes it easy to pour oil into one engine. You don't even have to hold the can.

4-10. Most oil fill caps are of the twist-off type installed in the engine top cover.

After you've added some oil—three quarts in the typical American car, two in the average import—check the engine's oil level. This is done by inspecting the dipstick. A car with automatic transmission has two dipsticks in the engine compartment, one for the engine oil, the other for the transmission oil (Fig. 4-11). You can tell the transmission oil dipstick from the engine dipstick in two ways:

(1) it is closer to the rear of the engine compartment than the engine dipstick;

(2) it comes out of a wider-diameter tube. This is because transmission oil is added through the dipstick tube, whereas engine oil is added through the fill hole.

Dipstick reading. To take an accurate dipstick reading, the car must be on reasonably level ground. Grasp the handle and pull out the dipstick from its tube. Wipe the oil off the tip of the dipstick, then reinsert it all the way. You may have to twist slightly to get it all the way down, so the base of the handle seats against the tube. Pull it out once more and read the level. Add half a quart of oil at a time, checking the dipstick reading after each addition, until the dipstick reads "full."

Final checks. Put on the oil cap, start the engine and let it idle for several minutes. Check the filter and the oil drain plug immediately, to see if there are any leaks. The odds are there will be no leaks, but if you spot a drip, stop the engine and find out why. It may simply be some oil you spilled on the engine as you were adding it, or the plug or filter may be loose and require additional tightening.

4-11.   Engines with automatic transmission have two dipsticks, one for engine oil (shown being pulled out) and another for transmission oil. Tube into which transmission oil dipstick fits is of noticeably larger diameter.

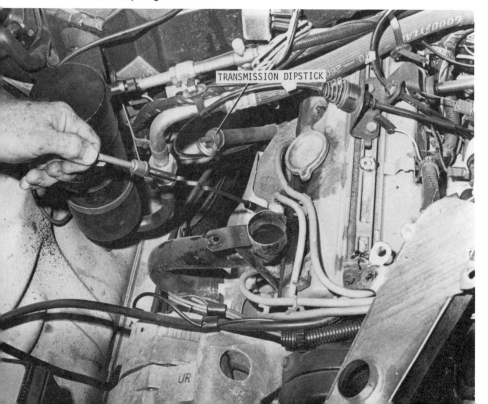

4-12. Grease plug may be used in joint instead of a fitting. If it is, remove with a wrench as shown, and install a grease fitting.

After five minutes of operation, stop the engine and allow two to three minutes for oil to drain into the oil pan. Take another dipstick reading and you'll probably find you must add some more oil. Reason: the oil filter holds up to a full quart; when it is filled by the engine's lubrication system the level in the oil pan is reduced. Top up as required to bring the dipstick level to full, and the job is done.

CHASSIS LUBRICATION. The term chassis lubrication is a misnomer, for what is really being lubricated are the suspension and steering systems. They have joints that flex up and down or side to side, and to minimize wear they require periodic injections of grease.

To permit grease to be injected, the joints have "fittings," which are little nipples with spring-loaded balls sealing them off. A grease gun, a tool that permits grease to be pumped under high pressure, pushes away the spring-loaded ball and grease enters the joint.

During the late 1960s some car manufacturers began threading small plugs (Fig. 4-12) into the joints. To lubricate the joint, the plug is removed and a grease gun with a special tip is used to inject the lubricant. For the weekend mechanic, however, a more practical approach is to remove the plugs and install permanent grease fittings in their place. Fittings are very inexpensive, costing only 15 to 25 cents each.

4-13. Lever-type grease gun is easiest to use. It is filled with a cartridge of grease that resembles tube of caulk. The tip of the nozzle fits on the tip of the grease fitting.

To grease the joints, you will need the following:

Grease gun. There are two types marketed for weekend mechanics: a pistol type and a lever design (Fig. 4-13). The lever type is easier to operate, particularly if it's necessary to build up high pressures on a slightly frozen grease fitting. Many grease fittings are so located that you can't reach them with the gun; therefore a flexible extension (Fig. 4-14) is necessary.

Grease. There is only one convenient way for you to buy grease: in a cartridge, like household caulk. As with other lubricants, stick with name brands. Choose a grease that is fortified with "moly" (molybdenum disulphide), a mineral product that contributes to the effective life of the lubricant.

44

Wrench, 5/16-inch. If a fitting is completely frozen (by rust and corrosion), the joint will not accept grease. The fitting must be replaced, using a 5/16-inch box or open-end wrench on the fitting's hexagonal surface. The wrench also can be used to remove plugs and install fittings in their place.

There are three basic locations for grease fittings:

On the car's front suspension. Typically, there is one fitting at each ball joint, which is a little swivel joint at the top and bottom of the suspension part to which

4-14.   If working angle is bad, a flexible nozzle should be used on the gun.

4-15. Conventional suspension has two ball joints at each wheel, and one grease fitting at each ball joint, as indicated by arrowheads.

the front wheel is attached (Fig. 4-15). Each car, therefore, has four ball joints. Exceptions are found among European and Japanese cars that have what is called a "strut" suspension, in which a spring and shock absorber are combined into a single unit. Here there is only one (lower) ball joint at each wheel, a total of two.

On the steering linkage. The steering linkage has several pivot points. Depending on the car, they all may be lubricated and sealed for life, or some or all may have fittings. Fig. 4-16 shows typical locations for grease fittings or plugs on late-model American cars. The chart shows the number of fittings on each make of car and where they are located.

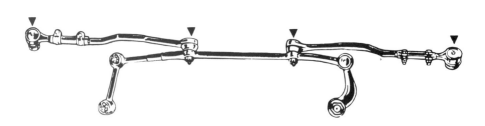

4-16. This is typical steering linkage. Arrowheads point to locations of grease fittings.

On the rear universal joint. On full-size General Motors cars, the rear universal joint of the propeller shaft (Fig. 4-17) has a special type of grease fitting. It is mounted flush inside the universal joint, which means it can only be greased with a special needle-tip adapter. The adapter available at auto parts stores that serve professional mechanics, is inexpensive and attaches to the tip of any grease-gun nozzle.

When you locate the grease fittings, wipe each one with a clean cloth. This will make them easier to spot and prevent dirt from being injected with the grease.

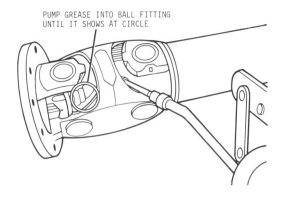

PUMP GREASE INTO BALL FITTING
UNTIL IT SHOWS AT CIRCLE

4-17. Rear universal joint on the propeller shaft of most full-size, late-model General Motors cars has a flush-type grease fitting. Ordinary nozzle won't fit on it, so you need a pencil-tip nozzle as shown. Inject grease into fitting until it just oozes out at circled area.

If the car has plugs instead of fittings, unthread the plugs with the 5/16 wrench, install and tighten the fittings. If a plug is so located that there is no room to install a conventional fitting, much less get a grease gun on it, you can install a right-angle grease fitting (Fig. 4-18). This type of fitting can be tightened in a position that will permit access with a grease gun.

Load the grease gun with the cartridge and attach the rigid nozzle. Push the nozzle tip onto the fitting—it will catch on the curved nipple of the fitting. Pump the lever and stop when you see some swelling on the rubber seal of the joint. On many cars there are grease bleed holes in the joints and you will see small amounts of grease extruding from them. This also tells you the joint is lubricated.

4-18. Right-angle grease fitting can be installed in a plug that is difficult to reach with a grease gun.

If a fitting does not take grease, the grease will just extrude from between the gun's nozzle tip and the fitting. Don't struggle. Remove the old fitting and install a replacement.

If a fitting is in an inaccessible location, remove the rigid nozzle and thread in the flexible one. Hold the tip of the flexible nozzle on the fitting if possible; this will position it properly and help with injection of grease.

Only full-size General Motors cars have a grease fitting on the propeller shaft, at the rear universal joint, but it's an important one and you might own such a car. Regular lubrication can extend the life of this joint.

Jack up the rear of the car and place safety stands under the rear-axle housing tubes and safety chocks at the front wheels, as explained in Chapter 2. Put the transmission in neutral and leave the parking brake off. Slip underneath and look at the rear universal joint. If you can see the grease fitting proceed to lubricate it. Insert the needle tip of the gun into the fitting, applying pressure to hold it in, and give the gun lever two or three short pumps.

If you can't see the fitting, turn one of the rear wheels, which will also turn the propeller shaft, until the fitting is accessible.

Note: If all you have are ramps, the job may be a bit more difficult. Position the ramps and back the rear wheels onto them, then apply the parking brake and put the transmission shift lever into Park (Reverse on a manual transmission). Slip underneath and see if the grease fitting is accessible. If it is, consider yourself fortunate and proceed to inject grease. If it isn't, drive the car off the ramps and forward several feet, move the ramps forward the same number of feet and back the car onto them once more. It may take several tries until the part of the universal joint with the grease fitting is exposed.

In addition to the parts with grease fittings or plugs, it is good practice to dab or smear grease onto all joints on the clutch linkage of manual transmission cars. You can find these joints by having a helper depress the clutch pedal while you look underneath. The moving part is the clutch linkage.

Do the same for the transmission linkage.

Complete the grease job by applying small amounts to door hinges, hood supports, and the hood release, plus trunk lid supports. This is more service than you would receive at a typical station.

MAKE OF CAR	STEERING LINKAGE	BALL JOINTS	OTHER
Chrysler Corp.	5	4	—
American Motors	2	4	—
Ford Motor Co.	4	4	—
Buick	7	4	a
Chevrolet	7	4	a
Pontiac	7	4	a
Olds Toronado	4	4	—
All other Olds	7	4	—
Cadillac Eldorado	5	4	—
All other Cadillacs	7	4	—

a. rear universal joint on full-size cars (except wagons) has flush grease fitting

5 | Basic Electrical Work

Many people are afraid of electricity, but when it comes to basic electrical work on a car, there's really nothing to worry about. Much of the work is done with the electricity shut off, and those few jobs that are performed with the juice flowing involve only 12 volts, which is about one-tenth of ordinary household current.

Two of the simple electrical jobs you can do on your car may save you big money—servicing battery terminals and charging a battery. Others—lamp replacements—may save you only a dollar or so. But by doing the work yourself you will avoid the inconvenience of making an appointment for service or waiting around in a shop until someone is free.

BATTERY TERMINALS. Periodic cleaning and tightening of battery terminals is one of the most important services you can perform on your car. The job takes just a few minutes and requires only two simple tools, but it can prevent starting failures and expensive emergency service.

To do the job you need:

Wire brush. You can buy one specially shaped for battery terminals (price $1 to $2). Perhaps you already have the spiral type (Fig. 5-1), called a plumber's brush, for household work.

5-1. Battery posts and inside of cable terminals can be cleaned effectively with a wire brush, either one made for the job or plumber's brush shown.

5-2. To remove spring-clamp battery terminal, squeeze ends together with pliers.

Wrench. For the cable terminals on the battery. An adjustable wrench is fine for those batteries with cylindrical posts on top, and may also work on the side terminal battery of all late-model General Motors cars. If the adjustable open-end wrench slips off the terminal retaining bolt, obtain a 5/16-inch wrench to do the job. If you have an older car, the cable terminals may have spring clamps. To release them, all you need are ordinary slip-joint pliers (Fig. 5-2).

Clean rags and baking soda. To remove oily road film from the top of the battery.

Disconnecting the cables. Begin by disconnecting the cables from the battery. The "ground" cable, the one that goes from the battery to a simple bolt-down on the body and/or nearby on the engine, should be disconnected first. Then take off the "live" cable, which goes to a terminal on either the starter or a relay (Fig. 5-3).

5-3. Short cable goes to the relay on this car; on others it goes directly to the starter. This is the "live" cable; the other one is connected to the engine and car body, and provides an electrical "ground." All other wiring in the car connected to the engine or car body is also grounded, and the engine or body metal becomes a return path to the battery to complete most electrical circuits in the car.

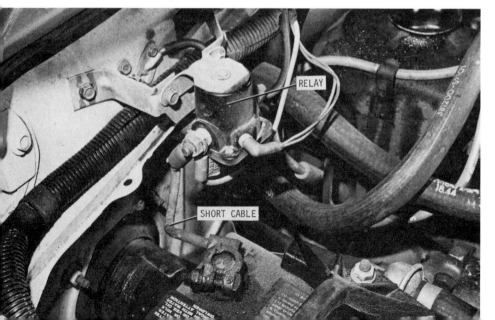

5-4. Hit cable terminal on side, back and forth, with hammer to loosen it. Or use an inexpensive terminal puller.

The actual disconnection technique varies as follows:

• *Battery with posts on top.* Slacken the nut that holds the cable terminal. Then twist the cable back and forth with an upward motion until it comes off. If it is really stuck, hit it back and forth with a hammer (Fig. 5-4) to work it free. In an extreme situation, obtain a battery terminal puller, available at all auto parts stores for $1 to $2.

• *Battery with side terminals.* Remove the retaining bolt and pull the cable terminal away.

• *Spring clamp cables.* Squeeze the ends together with pliers, and using the pliers as a handle, twist the cable back and forth to free it. With your other hand, hold the other end of the terminal (where it joins with the wire) and apply lifting pressure at the same time. If the terminal is really stuck, use a battery terminal puller. Keep the ends of the clamp squeezed together with the pliers as you turn the forcing screw on the puller.

Cleaning up. On top-post designs, clean the entire surface of the post and both the inside and outside of the terminal. On batteries with side terminals, brush both contact surfaces (Fig. 5-5), making sure your brush hits the crevices. The whitish or greenish-white corrosion deposits are obvious and you surely will do a careful job of removing them, but all surfaces should be clean and brightened, not just those with the deposits.

Next, make up a solution of baking soda and water (1 tablespoon to a glass of water) and with a cloth remove all road film from the top of the battery.

Inspect the hold-down, the bracket that keeps the battery firmly in place. If it is corroded, unbolt it from the battery box and wire-brush it clean. Spray the threaded parts (nuts, hold-down screws, bolts, etc.) with penetrating oil.

If the corrosion deposits on the hold-down bracket are substantial and really ate into it, replace the part with one that is plastic-coated for longer life. If you got to the hold-down before it was eaten away, paint it with corrosion-resistant paint and reinstall.

If the corrosion has really eaten into both the hold-down and the battery box, remove the battery, wire-brush the entire box too, and spray both box and hold-down (if still salvageable) with an aerosol paint made for battery boxes. It's available in auto parts stores.

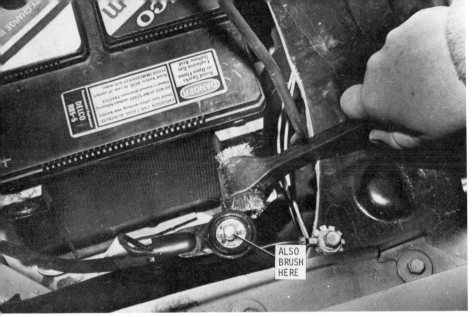

5-5. On side-terminal battery, clean both contact faces with a brush—one on battery, the other on the inside face of the cable terminal.

Refitting the cables. Once everything is clean, replace the cable terminals on the battery. On the top-post type, tighten the nut until you have to apply moderate force. The terminal should be tight enough so you cannot twist it. If you can twist the terminal, give the nut another half-turn and try again. If that doesn't do it, inspect the terminal. You may find that the tips of the terminal jaws are squeezed together and there is really no use to tighten them further. There are three possible cures:

(1) Replace the cable terminal (explained later in this chapter).

(2) Remove the nut and bolt from the terminal and cut off the tips of the jaws with a hacksaw.

(3) Slacken the nut, twist the terminal back and forth until it is free, then wedge in a thin strip of metal (cut to size) between post and terminal. The strip acts as a shim and when you tighten the nut once more the attachment should be very secure.

Got a good connection? Complete the job by coating the terminal and top of the post with petroleum jelly to retard corrosion.

On spring clamp terminals, squeeze the ends together to expand the clamp, push down onto the battery post and release the grip with the pliers. Try to twist the terminal, and if it can be turned in either direction, the terminal should be replaced, as explained later in this chapter.

On side terminal batteries, position the terminal on the battery, refit the retaining bolt and tighten. It should not take a great deal of tightening to achieve a good connection. However, if you encounter erratic engine cranking, give the bolt a quarter-turn more and see if the problem is cured.

Replacing a terminal. Replacement terminals for top-post cables are more readily available than those for side-terminal cables. This is probably because of the low failure rate of the side-terminal cables compared to the top-post design. Also, top-post cables represent far greater volume because they have been used for so many years.

If a top-post terminal is badly corroded or no longer fits properly, it can be replaced. The best procedure would be to change the entire cable, which is not expensive. If you can get a wrench on the far end of the cable and disconnect it, you can then install a new cable. On most Ford cars, for example, the battery cables are short and replacing them is easy (Fig. 5-3). The same is true of the ground cable on most cars. The far end(s) are generally accessible. However, a split cable design may not be inexpensive, so you will have to measure cost vs. the effort involved in installing only a new terminal.

There is commonly an access problem with the live cable to the starter. In fact, the cable may disappear into a harness with other wiring and pose a real problem. In this case, installing only a new terminal is the quick and economical solution. Auto parts stores generally carry two grades of terminals: very cheap and moderately cheap. Neither will enjoy particularly long life, but once you make the installation, putting in a replacement will take just minutes. Buy the more expensive terminal; it is plated to retard corrosion.

To install the new terminal, remove the old one with a hacksaw, strip off a half-inch of insulation at the end of the wire, using a razor blade, and brush off any corrosion on the exposed end of the wire conductor.

With a wrench if necessary, slacken the nuts and bolts that clamp the curved retaining plate to the terminal, push the wire in, between retaining plate and terminal, and tighten the nuts and bolts securely (Fig. 5-6). The terminal is now ready for installation.

5-6.   Replacement terminal is attached to the battery cable with a clamping plate held by two screws. Here one screw is being given final tightening after the terminal has been connected to the battery.

5-7. To check the drive belt, press down midway between pulleys as shown. Belt should not deflect more than 3/4 inch.

BATTERY CHARGING. If a battery constantly runs down in normal operation, the problem usually is in one of these five areas:

(1) An electrical problem called a short circuit.

(2) A defect in the charging system. Either a bad alternator (AC current generator) or a loose drive belt, usually the same belt that operates the water pump and fan.

(3) A defective battery (including failure to top up with water).

(4) Bad cable connections.

(5) Short-trip driving, which does not give the charging system the necessary time to recharge the battery.

There is a sixth cause that we all encounter: leaving the lights on with the engine off.

If a problem in the charging system is severe, the dashboard warning lamp will go on. A loose drive belt can be checked simply by pressing down on it about 6 inches from the alternator pulley (Fig. 5-7). If the belt deflects more than 3/4 inch under thumb pressure, it is loose and must be readjusted. If the belt feels tight, that is not the problem.

Defective cable connections are a problem you can now diagnose and correct.

Whether you can isolate the cause of the problem or not is often immaterial. If you can get the battery charged and the engine running, it will cost you less money than if you call for a tow truck.

To charge a battery completely, you need a piece of equipment called a battery charger, and the type most suitable for home mechanics is a trickle charger, which means that it just sends a trickle of current into the battery. It may take up to forty-eight hours to recharge a battery with a small trickle charger, although charging adequate to start a car may be accomplished in six to eight hours.

Trickle chargers come in many sizes and in a wide range of prices. The smallest, a two-amp charger, may be purchased from discount houses during a sale for well under $10 (see Fig. 5-8).

5-8. Trickle charger is shown in use. Alligator clips connect it to battery; then it is plugged into household current.

To use the charger, just turn the switch to 12 (volts; all cars today have 12-volt batteries), connect the clip from the red wire to the live terminal to the relay or starter; and the other wire, usually green or black, to the ground terminal. If both wires are black, the clips will have colored insulators on the handles. You can connect the clips to the cable terminals; but on top-post batteries you can remove the cables and connect directly to the battery posts. On side terminal batteries, you can charge with the cables removed by simply threading the bolts into the terminals and attaching the charger clips to the bolts. These techniques are used when the car has conked out in a location that does not permit connecting a charger into household current, and the battery therefore must be removed from the car.

Before you actually begin charging, make sure there is an adequate amount of water in each cell. Remove the caps and, if necessary, add water to bring the level to above the plates. Leave the caps off during the charging.

Boost-starting. To boost-start a car from another car's battery, you need booster cables, available in auto supply stores and even some supermarkets. Line up the cars so the cables reach from one battery to the next, making sure the bumpers do not touch. Locate the live terminal to the relay or starter on each battery and connect one cable to that terminal on each car. Then connect the other two terminals.

Note: As a safety precaution, the caps should be removed before boost-starting. It is also a safe procedure to make the final booster cable connection (spanning the terminals that don't go to the starter or relay) to a bolt on the engine at least a foot away from the battery.

Start and run the engine of the car with the good battery; after a minute, attempt to start the car with the dead battery.

Once the car with the dead battery is started, the charging system will immediately take over and provide current to keep the ignition system of the engine functioning, and recharge the battery. If the engine immediately stalls, and does this repeatedly, the problem is in the charging system. If the battery is recharged with a trickle charger for a sufficient period, it will have enough current to start the car and permit it to be driven to a repair shop.

REPLACING EXTERIOR BULBS. Replacing exterior bulbs is simple work on most cars. The most difficult part of the job for many people is to obtain the correct replacement bulb. To be sure you buy the correct bulb, remove the defective bulb and take it with you to the store. Check the new bulb to be sure that it is the same shape, that it has the same number of terminals on the bottom, either one or two, and that the locking tips on the side are in the same position.

Most rear lamps can be reached through the trunk compartment. When you lift the trunk lid you should see the back of the socket. Twist it to release the locking tangs; then pull it straight out.

To disengage the bulb, gently grasp the circular glass envelope, push the bulb down into the socket and twist it counterclockwise until it stops (a quarter inch or so). Release downward pressure and the bulb will rise and can be lifted out. If the socket is badly corroded from water, the bulb may stick in the socket. Spray in some penetrating solvent, which is sold in aerosol cans, often with a straw to permit a pinpointing spray. Allow several minutes for the solvent to work, then try again. Do not apply excessive force to the bulb's envelope or it may break.

Installing the new bulb is just a matter of reversing the procedure. First, look at the inside of the socket; you'll see slots for the bulb's locking tips. Insert the bulb so the tips slide in the slots, then push down and twist. If the bulb won't turn, you probably have a high tip in the long slot and the low tip in the short slot. Remove the bulb and rotate 180 degrees.

Other small lamps. The basic procedure for rear lamps should work for all, although access may not be as convenient. Many small front lamps are reached from under the hood or from behind a fender. On some cars access to the bulb may be directly in front, under the covering lens (Fig. 5-9). If you can't see any other access and the lens is held by screws, remove them and pull off the lens. It

5-9. If there's no obvious access to bulb from the back, and lens is held by screws, remove the lens.

5-10. If you can't grasp the bulb with your fingers, use a flexible plastic bulb extractor.

is not uncommon for the bulb to project a short distance from the surface of the socket, and you may not be able to get a good grip on it. If you cannot, buy a bulb extracting tool kit (Fig. 5-10). The soft plastic or rubber cup will extract the bulb and reduce danger of breakage.

Sometimes the covering lens is not held by screws and there is no access from behind. A trim molding may be holding the lens. This isn't unusual with the direction indicator signals on the tops of fenders, and it can take a professional an hour to get the molding off, change the bulb, and replace the molding. If you don't know how to change the bulb, give the job to a professional and watch him.

Testing a bulb. Usually you can see the burned-out filament in a dead bulb. If you're not sure, you can test the bulb, using the car's battery and a piece of wire (Fig. 5-11). Just lay the bulb on its side so the metal portion is agianst the ground terminal of the battery. Tie one end of the wire around the live terminal. Touch the other end of the wire to the silver metal nipple on the base of the bulb. A live bulb should light. If the bulb has two filaments, it will have two nipples. Touching the wire to each one will light the filament to which it is connected.

5-11. To test the bulb, rest the side on the ground cable post of the battery and with a wire attached to a live terminal, touch the end to the terminal on the base of the bulb. This bulb has two filaments, therefore two terminals at the base, and they're checked separately.

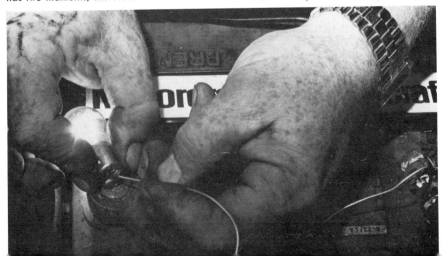

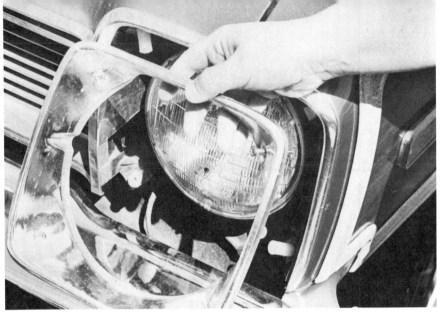

5-12. Headlamp molding is held by screws; remove them and gently pry off the molding.

Headlamps. You can change a burned-out headlamp without disturbing the aim. It just takes a little care.

First, determine access to the headlamp. On most cars the lamp is recessed behind a molding held by screws. Remove the screws, pry off the molding with a screwdriver, and you're ready to start (Fig. 5-12). On some late-model American cars, the headlamp molding is of soft plastic and there is enough clearance, or cutout slots, to permit you to reach the retaining screws with a thin screwdriver. On some foreign cars there is a trim ring around the outer edge of the headlamp. Just slip a thin screwdriver under it at two opposite points, pry forward, and it will spring off.

5-13. Three screws go through a retaining rim and two don't. The ones that don't are aiming screws and shouldn't be disturbed. Remove the other screws with a screwdriver.

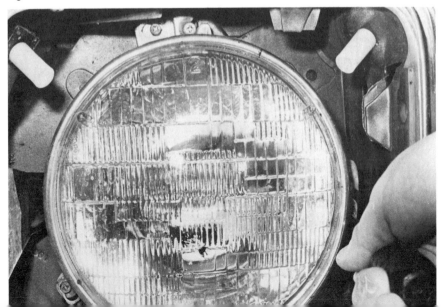

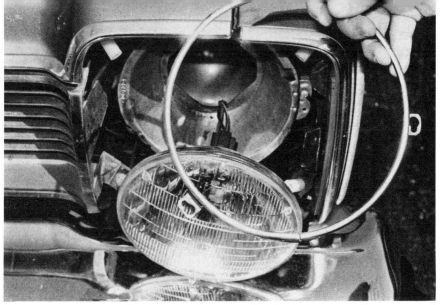

5-14. Retaining rim is off and the headlamp is pulled forward.

Once you have access to the headlamp, you will see three screws that hold it in place (Figs. 5-13 and 5-14). There are two additional screws with tiny coil springs, one at the top and the second at one side. These latter two are the aim adjusting screws and should not be disturbed. Remove the three retaining screws. If they are rusty or corroded and you have difficulty, spray them with penetrating solvent first (Fig. 5-15). Do not force the screws, for you might damage the heads. Have patience, apply penetrating solvent generously, and they'll come out. Make sure the screwdriver is the correct size.

Once the screws are out, you can pull the headlamp forward along with the retaining ring (Fig. 5-16). Reach behind the headlamp and pull of the wire connec-

5-15. If screws are rusted in place, spray with penetrating solvent. This brand has an aiming straw for getting into tight places.

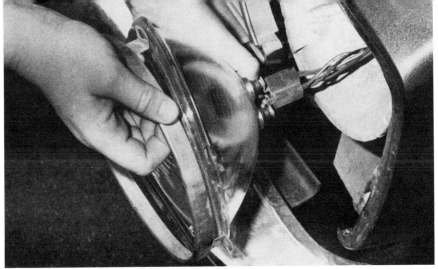

5-16. When screws have been removed, the headlamp and retaining ring can be pulled forward. The connecting terminal can be seen in this side view.

tor (Fig. 5-17). Attach the connector to the new headlamp. Now you can replace the headlamp. Just one caution: The headlamp has a top and a bottom, even though it's round. The number on the headlamp lens should be vertical, not upside down.

Testing a headlamp. If a headlamp fails to light, the cause may be a wiring problem. It is therefore a good idea to test the headlamp before purchasing a replacement.

Remove the headlamp, and as you remove the wiring connector observe which terminal on the back of the headlamp is connected to the black wire. Take the headlamp to the car battery and attach a jumper wire to each battery terminal. Clip the one from the ground terminal (the one whose cable is just bolted to the car body and the engine) to the lamp terminal that was connected to the black wire. Connect the other jumper wire to one of the other terminals, then switch it to the final terminal. If the headlamp is good, it will light each time you connect the second jumper wire to a terminal. If it lights on only one terminal (something it will also have done on the car), one of the filaments is burned out.

You can similarly test a headlamp on a four-lamp system, but there are only two terminals on the back of the lamp, for each lamp has only one filament, and therefore you have to make only one test.

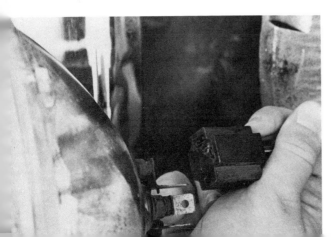

5-17. To replace headlamp, pull off connecting terminal.

6 | Introduction to the Tune-up

If you drive a car, you surely have heard that it periodically needs an engine tune-up, but you may not know what a tune-up is. In a sense, you have a lot of company, for no two professional mechanics or automotive engineers could define the term precisely. Tune-up is a catch-all term for services that improve engine performance. Yet rarely do these services actually involve the engine. Rather, they are normally performed on components that are bolted to the engine, which means that you never have to get "into" the engine itself to service them.

This chapter will introduce you to the services that are common to most basic tune-ups, the parts you need and how to buy them, and what tools are required.

SPARK PLUGS. These are the terminal parts of the ignition system. They are threaded into holes at the tops of the cylinders, into the part of the engine called the cylinder head (Fig. 6-1). There is customarily one spark plug for each cylinder.

The ignition system produces high-voltage electricity and sends it through a wire to the spark plug when the fuel mixture in the cylinder is ready to be ignited. The electricity goes from the wire to a metal rod that passes through the center of the spark plug (Fig. 6-2). It gets to the end of the rod and has nowhere to

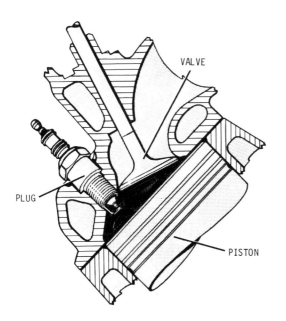

6-1. Spark plug threads into a hole at the top of the cylinder.

VALVE

PLUG

PISTON

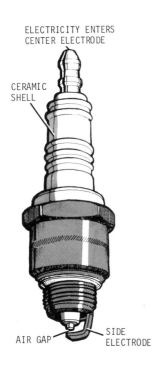

ELECTRICITY ENTERS
CENTER ELECTRODE

CERAMIC
SHELL

AIR GAP — SIDE ELECTRODE

6-2. How a spark plug works: High-voltage electricity from the plug wire enters at the center electrode, which protrudes through an insulating ceramic shell. Electricity flows down the center electrode and jumps the air gap to the side electrode, causing a spark.

continue. To complete its circuit—which electricity must do—it must return to its source (although depleted of its energy).

On an automobile the electrical ground is the method used to provide a return path for electricity. The battery is the source and one of its cables is attached to the car body and to the engine. Therefore, any wire that is connected to the engine or the car body completes a circuit back to the battery.

The spark plug has an L-shaped strip of metal on the side that is attached to the threaded section, so the strip is grounded to the engine. The electricity jumps from the center rod (which is called the center electrode) to that side strip (which is called the side electrode). It is the electricity jumping the air gap between the two electrodes that forms what we call the spark, and it ignites the fuel mixture.

The gap between the two electrodes must be precisely right. If it is too wide, the ignition system may not be able to produce enough electrical pressure—voltage—to enable the electricity to jump the gap. If it is too small, the spark is too short to set the fuel mixture afire.

Spark plugs wear out. Electricity erodes the tips of the electrodes, widening the gap. Deposits from the burning of the fuel mixture coat all internal parts of the spark plugs, and they form electrically conductive paths for the electricity. Instead of jumping the gap and creating a spark, the electricity takes the easier road, along one of the paths formed by the deposits.

Spark plugs can be cleaned and the gap readjusted, but the results are not nearly as satisfactory as installing new plugs, and the investment in cleaning equipment cannot be justified by a weekend mechanic. Therefore, replacing the spark plugs once a year or every 15,000 miles is considered good preventive maintenance.

POINTS AND CONDENSER. The points, more completely referred to as the breaker or ignition points, are an electric switch inside the distributor (Fig. 6-3). They open and close on a regular schedule mechanically designed into the engine. Voltage builds up in the ignition coil, which is a type of high-voltage electrical transformer, and when a spark plug needs the electricity to fire the fuel mixture, the engine opens the points. This causes the coil to instantly discharge high-voltage electricity. The current flows from the center of the coil through a wire, into a cap on top of the distributor. It is transferred to a part called a rotor, which distributes it to the correct spark plug wire, as shown in Fig. 6-3.

Some of the electricity tries to arc across the ignition points, and if it were allowed, the points would be burned in short order. To prevent this, the condenser is used. It is an electrical shock absorber that accepts stray high voltage from the coil when the points are opened. When the points close, the condenser discharges the current through them to electrical ground, completing a circuit.

Although the condenser absorbs virtually all the stray high voltage, the breaker points are still subject to some current passage, and eventually their contact faces do burn. Therefore, the points should be replaced at the same time as the spark plugs. It is customary to replace the condenser at the same time as the points, and many replacement sets of points have a condenser built in (Fig. 6-4).

Newer cars have electronic ignition (Chrysler products since 1973, other American cars since 1975), which eliminates the points and condenser. Transistorized circuitry does their job. On the overwhelming majority of cars on the road, however, points and condenser are used.

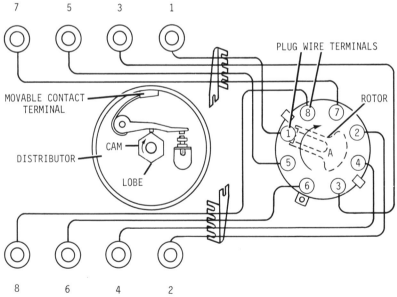

6-3. Simple drawing shows how the ignition system works. A cam in the distributor is turned by the engine, and when the lobe comes against the block of the movable contact arm, it pushes the movable contact away from the fixed contact, breaking the circuit and causing the ignition coil (not shown) to discharge. The coil discharges high-voltage electricity to the center of the distributor cap at point A. Electricity enters the cap and is transferred to the rotor, which is mounted on top of cam, and is also spun by the engine. When the rotor tip aligns with the plug wire terminal, it transfers high-voltage electricity to the terminal, from where it flows to the spark-plug wire and from the wire into the plug. Not shown is the condenser, which is mounted in the distributor and connected to the movable contact terminal.

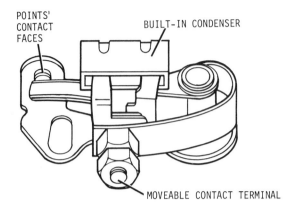

POINTS'
CONTACT
FACES

BUILT-IN CONDENSER

MOVEABLE CONTACT TERMINAL

6-4.   Combination breaker points and condenser.

Replacement points are not merely installed; they are also adjusted. When they are opened by the engine, the two contact faces must separate a precise distance. If they are adjusted so the gap is too small, they will open too late and the spark at the plugs will occur too late for efficient car performance. If they are adjusted so the gap is too great, they will open too early, also affecting engine performance. Because their gap affects the timing of the spark (called ignition timing), they must be adjusted before making what is called an ignition timing check.

Ignition timing. The arrival of the spark at the plug must be a precisely timed event that coincides with the fuel mixture being compressed to the maximum by the piston. For the greater the compression of the mixture, the greater is the power developed when it ignites and explodes.

As explained, the opening of the breaker points in the distributor causes the ignition coil to discharge. Because of the speed of electricity, the opening of the points can also be considered the time of ignition.

To determine if the timing of the spark is correct, the car maker provides reference marks on the engine for No. 1 cylinder (if timing is right for one cylinder, it's right for all). One mark is on the crankshaft belt pulley, the other is on a stationary indicator on the front the engine (Fig. 6-5). A tool called a timing light is connected to the No. 1 cylinder's spark plug. As the current passes through the plug wire to the plug, it triggers the timing light, turning it on. The light is aimed at the reference marks, and if they are aligned when the light goes on, timing is correct.

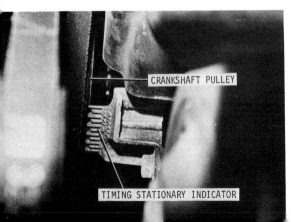

CRANKSHAFT PULLEY

TIMING STATIONARY INDICATOR

6-5.   This is a typical timing-mark arrangement on American cars. The stationary indicator has degree markings. The crankshaft pulley has a notch in the rim. When No. 1 spark plug fires, the notch should align with the correct mark on the stationary indicator.

If the marks are not aligned, timing is adjusted by turning the distributor body. This changes the instant at which the breaker points open, therefore changing the timing of the spark at the plugs.

IDLE SPEED. When you step on the gas pedal, the engine speeds up; remove your foot and it slows down. The slowest speed at which the engine will run satisfactorily is called idle speed or curb idle. If the speed is too low, the engine may stall repeatedly; if it's too high, the engine will waste gas and certain parts of the car will be strained. The linkage from the gas pedal to the carburetor has a provision for adjustment to idle speed—at the carburetor. The idle speed is measured with an electrical instrument called a tachometer.

AIR FILTER. An engine really runs on air—10 to 18 parts of air for each part of gasoline. That air must be free of abrasive dirt, for if dirt gets into the engine it causes excessive wear on many precision parts. All air contains some abrasive dirt, and because the engine uses so much air, a filter must be used to insure that the air supply is really clean.

The filter is mounted on top of the carburetor, where the air enters. The filter, generally made of a heat-cured, resin-impregnated cellulose (called "paper"), removes virtually all dirt particles of significant size before they can reach the engine. The filter is in a sheet metal or plastic housing, and access to it is normally by removal of a cover on top of the housing.

The life of an air filter depends on the amount of dirt in the air. The filter may last 25,000 miles or more; it may last 10,000 miles or less. On almost all cars the filter can be removed from the housing and inspected. If it appears dirty, it is replaced.

On a few cars the filter is inside a sealed cannister. In this case there is no way to check it. The factory recommendation is for replacement at five years or 50,000 miles, but two years or 25,000 miles is a prudent maximum.

COMPRESSION TEST. Before you can expect to get good results from the services included in a tune-up, you must be sure the engine is in basically good mechanical condition. There is one test that is customarily used to evaluate the engine mechanically—the compression test.

This test, performed with the spark plugs removed, consists of inserting a pressure gauge into a spark plug hole (Fig. 6-6), cranking the engine and measuring

6-6. Compression gauge is pressed into the spark plug hole to measure the pressure that develops when the engine is cranking. The gauge provides an indication of the engine's general mechanical condition.

6-7. Feeler gauges are either strips of metal or pieces of wire of a calibrated thickness. Gauge shown, which is for spark plugs, has six U-shaped pieces of wire of different thicknesses, to check the gap on spark plugs in cars with electronic ignition.

the pressure developed in the cylinder. The pressure is provided by the piston rising in the cylinder and squeezing the air into a tiny space just above it. This space, called the combustion chamber, is where the spark plug ignites the mixture. The closer the pressure is to normal, the greater is the force of the explosion when the plug fires the fuel mixture. If the pressure developed in any one, several or all cylinders is low, the engine will not perform satisfactorily, even with new spark plugs and other tune-up service. Low pressure means there is a malfunction, and the engine should be checked and serviced by a professional mechanic.

TOOLS FOR TUNE-UP. To do a tune-up you need special equipment. It isn't very expensive, and it will pay for itself with the first job. Here's what you need, why you need it and where to buy it.

Feeler Gauge. This is an assortment of strips of wire or flat metal of precisely calibrated thickness, used to measure the air gap between the electrodes of spark plugs and the contact faces of ignition points (when they are open). To use the gauge, select the wire or strip of metal of factory-specified thickness and insert it in the gap. It should go in and out with light-to-moderate drag. You can "feel" the gap with the gauge. Wire gauges are used for spark plugs; flat gauges for ignition points (Fig. 6-7).

You can buy sets of feeler gauges in almost any place that carries auto parts. A combination set (for both plugs and points) costs between $3 and $10.

Be careful when you buy. To cover all late-model cars, including those with electronic ignition, you need a set of spark-plug wire gauges with the following thicknesses: .025 inch, .035, .040, .045, .050, .060, and .080. Many gauges only go as high as .040 inch.

The flat metal feeler gauges for ignition points are available in two designs: single thickness for each metal strip and dual thickness with a step at the point the thickness changes. This second type, called a "go–no-go" gauge, is more expensive but is easier for a beginner to use. If you are trying to gauge an air gap of .019 inch, you would select a gauge marked .018–.020 inch. The first part of the gauge should fit in (the .018 inch), the second part should not. This tells you that the gap is at least .018 inch wide, but not .020 inch wide. That means it must be .019 inch wide, which is what you are trying to get.

Spark plug socket. A spark plug has a hexagonal section at its midpoint to receive a wrench. A standard socket won't be deep enough to reach that hex section, so a special deep socket is used. The deep socket made for spark plug service often contains a magnet or a sponge to hold the plug in place in the socket (Fig. 6-8). If you already have obtained a socket and ratchet set in a 3/8-inch drive, as discussed in Chapter 2, and the spark plug socket was not included, make sure the socket you buy, is also 3/8 drive, so you can use the ratchet and extension rods with that set.

A spark plug socket costs only a few dollars and can be purchased anywhere automotive parts are sold. Take along a spark plug to get the right size.

Plug cleaner. As an engine accumulates mileage, the burning of combustion gases may permit some carbon deposits to accumulate in on the threads at the base of the spark-plug and those in the hole. If the spark plug is difficult to remove, clean the threaded area of the hole with a special cleaning tool. It costs a few dollars, but is sold only in those auto parts stores that serve the professional mechanic.

Compression gauge. This gauge is made in several forms. The simplest and least expensive is the type shown in Fig. 6-6. You insert it in the spark-plug hole and exert pressure while a helper cranks the engine. If the spark-plug holes all are not accessible, you can use a gauge with a long hose that threads into the hole and eliminates the need to hold the gauge. This also means you can crank the engine yourself.

Note: If your spark-plug holes are all accessible, you can also do the test yourself with a remote starter switch. This is a pushbutton with long wires that connects to the starter and battery. It can be held and operated with one hand while you hold the gauge in place with the other.

The hand-held compression gauge is $4 and up; the remote starter switch is $5 and up. A compression gauge with a hose is $15 and up. You can buy the first two items in a set with other tools described in this chapter, but the other tools included, particularly the timing light, are usually not the type you really need. Sources of supply for the first two tools are any place that sells automotive parts. The compression gauge with the long hose may be purchased by mail order or at parts stores that serve professional mechanics.

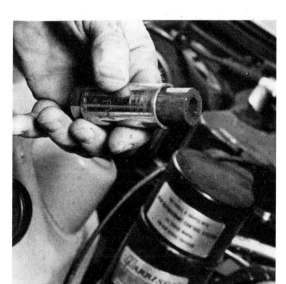

6-8. This is a spark-plug socket. Notice that it is deeper than an ordinary socket. Observe the sponge-rubber insert that has been partly pulled out. It is designed to hold the plug in the socket.

Timing light. There are three basic types of timing lights: neon tube, AC power, and DC power. The neon tube design, included in many tune-up tool kits sold to weekend mechanics, is only connected to the No. 1 spark plug wire, not to the car battery. The light it emits is very dim and so it must be held very close to the timing marks. This usually is not possible because of clearance problems in engine compartments. The light also must be used in virtual darkness.

Although the neon-tube light is very cheap (often available for less than $5), it is really unsatisfactory.

The AC light is satisfactory, because it uses AC current to provide a bright light you can see under all conditions. The light is also connected to the No. 1 spark plug wire, but the spark plug current only has to trigger the light. At about $20, the AC-power timing light is the least expensive model, but it must be plugged into household current, making it somewhat inconvenient to use. For just a few dollars more, you can obtain one of the lower priced 12-volt DC timing lights, which connects to the car battery and also emits a bright, clear light. You don't need a professional mechanic's version in a bright chrome housing; a plastic housing will be satisfactory for the occasional use you will give the tool. There are many different models; the most significant feature is the method of attachment to the No. 1 spark-plug wire. One of the three following attachments is common.

• In series with the plug wire and the plug (Fig. 6-9). You disconnect the plug wire and fit a coil spring over the end of the plug and into the terminal of the plug wire, then attach an alligator clip on the timing light wire to the spring. Although

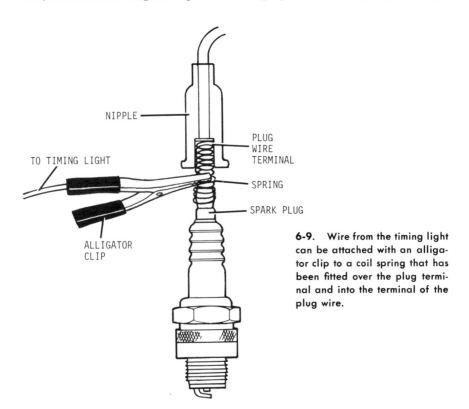

NIPPLE

PLUG WIRE TERMINAL

TO TIMING LIGHT

SPRING

SPARK PLUG

ALLIGATOR CLIP

6-9. Wire from the timing light can be attached with an alligator clip to a coil spring that has been fitted over the plug terminal and into the terminal of the plug wire.

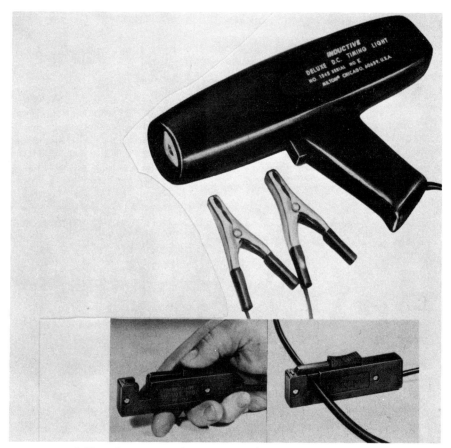

6-10. This is a timing light with an inductive pickup trigger wire that just clamps over the spark-plug wire at any point.

this type is the least expensive, it may be somewhat inconvenient if the No. 1 plug is in an inaccessible location.

• In series with the plug wire and the distributor cap. You disconnect the plug wire from the cap and fit a special adapter from the trigger wire into the cap and over the plug wire. Although this is easier to connect than the previous design (and slightly more expensive), it won't work on late-model General Motors cars with electronic ignition. New timing lights that will also work with the GM electronic ignition distributor are planned for introduction soon.

• Clip onto the spark-plug wire. The clip is a special electronic device that attaches to the plug wire rubber jacket. There are two designs, one called capacitive pickup, the other called inductive pickup. The capacitive is cheaper, but it will not work with all types of electronic ignition. If you buy this type, and it's the most convenient (Fig. 6-10), be sure it has what is called an inductive pickup.

Prices of power timing lights start at under $20 (in a discount house during a sale) and go as high as over $50. If you are looking for a premium model, such as a DC power type with an inductive pickup, shop at stores that also serve professional mechanics, and check mail order sources. The discount house is unlikely to carry the more expensive designs.

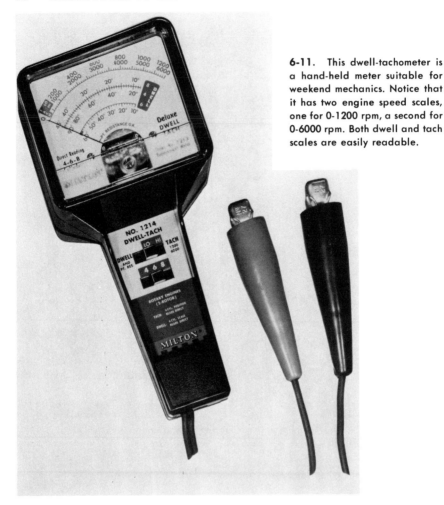

6-11. This dwell-tachometer is a hand-held meter suitable for weekend mechanics. Notice that it has two engine speed scales, one for 0-1200 rpm, a second for 0-6000 rpm. Both dwell and tach scales are easily readable.

Dwell Tachometer. A tachometer is a test instrument that measures engine speed. It is connected to the ignition coil or the terminal from the ignition points in the distributor, where it is operated by ignition voltage, which it converts into an engine speed figure.

The tachometer is customarily combined with a dwellmeter, an instrument that measures the time the breaker points are closed. When the points are closed there is no spark, but this interval is significant because the coil is charging up.

Dwell is the time the points are closed as measured in degrees, and it is effectively the opposite of the points open. If dwell is correct, so is the gap to which the points open, providing a double check on a point's adjustment.

Both dwellmeter and tachometer are connected the same way, so when they are combined into a single meter (Fig. 6-11), all that's necessary is to flip a switch to get one reading or the other.

There are two important considerations in choosing a dwell-tachometer:

(1) the meter scale must be wide enough to read accurately, to within 1 degree on the dwell scale, to within 50 revolutions per minute (rpm) on the engine speed scale;

(2) the engine speed portion of the meter face must have the most useful scales. For all tune-up work you need one low-reading scale, such as 0-1000, 0-1500, or 0-2000 rpm. If there is a high-reading scale, such as 0-5000 or higher, that may be useful if you go into advanced troubleshooting.

Dwell-tachometers can be obtained almost everywhere automotive parts are sold, including mail-order houses. There are meters for as low as $15, but for one with suitable scales, expect to pay at least double that.

Combination meter. A useful item is a meter that covers dwell and engine speed, and has a built-in timing light (Fig. 6-12). Price: $40 to $75. It may be available in some discount houses, but the more likely sources are mail order houses or auto parts stores serving the professional mechanic.

Ohmmeter. This is a meter that measures resistance to the flow of electricity, in units called ohms. It has three tune-up uses: to check a key part of the electronic ignition system; to check a part called a resistor; and to test spark-plug wires. If your car doesn't have electronic ignition, hold off buying an ohmmeter. If it does, buy one with a full range of scales: 0-50, 0-500, 0-5000, 0-50,000, and 0-500,000 ohms. Actually the meter may have only one scale, plus a knob that is turned to multiply the readings (Fig. 6-13). Price: $35 and up.

6-12. This is a combination dwell-tachometer-timing light. It provides all meter functions in one unit.

6-13. This is an ohmmeter with a full range of scales. Any automotive reading you take with it will be accurate.

Distributor wrench. The distributor is held in position by a little bracket and locking bolt or nut. This bolt or nut must be loosened in order to turn the distributor body when adjusting breaker points and ignition timing. An ordinary open-end, box, or socket wrench may do, but often you need a C-shaped box wrench to fit the locking bolt or nut. The wrench, which costs a few dollars, is sold in auto parts stores or by mail order, but rarely in discount houses.

Allen wrench. This is a wrench with a hexagonal-shaped working tip that fits into a hex-shaped recess in the screw head. Allen screws are becoming more popular on cars, for use in tight working quarters. You will find 1/8-inch Allen wrench necessary to adjust the breaker points on General Motors V-8 distributors and the idle speed on some newer GM cars. When shopping, look for an Allen wrench specifically recommended for GM V-8 distributors. It will be designed for easy access on point adjustments and idle speed settings.

BUYING PARTS. Routine parts (points, condensers, plugs, air filters) are sold in almost any place that sells auto parts. Avoid unknown brands, however, even if the price is attractive. Many low-cost parts do not fit well or perform properly.

You can buy parts individually or in sets that include plugs, points, condenser, and perhaps some other parts. Although the sets are a more economical buy if you need all the parts they contain, they frequently include items that are replaced only once every few years, such as spark-plug wires and the distributor rotor. You should expect at least a 40 percent discount from list price on ignition parts and the air filter, perhaps as much as 60 percent (particularly on spark plugs).

6-14. To determine how many barrels a carburetor has, remove the air cleaner and count the number of large individual holes. This carburetor has four (each labeled B).

Depending on where you live, the best prices may be found in discount houses, but you will have to read the manufacturers' catalogs in order to pick out the parts you need. Many manufacturers now list important information about the part on the back of the carton. In order to buy the correct parts, you should know the following:

• Year.
• Model.
• Engine type (4, 6, 8 cylinders).
• Displacement in cubic inches or liters. This is a measurement of the total volume of all the cylinders. You will generally need to know this information in order to set ignition timing, check compression, buy spark plugs and air filter, and in many instances, to buy the breaker points and condenser.
• Number of carburetor barrels. You probably have heard of one-barrel, two-barrel, and four-barrel carburetors. The term refers to the number of air holes in the carburetor. Just remove the air cleaner cover (Fig. 6-14) and count the number of large holes.

Catalog listings. If you have never read an auto parts catalog before, the listings may be confusing. You must find the one that is completely descriptive of your car. Let's use as an example a 1973 Dodge Coronet with a 360 cubic-inch v-8 and two-barrel carburetor. The catalog might read:

1968-76	All six-cylinder	4725-S
1968-72	318 V-8, 360 V-8, all models	4815-D
1973-74	360 V-8 two-barrel Charger, Monaco	4816-F
	360 V-8 two-barrel, all other models	4816-G
1968-72	360 V-8 four-barrel, all models	4818-M
1968-76	All other V-8s	4819-R

The correct part number is not 4815-D, because that number was used on 360 V-8s only up through 1972. It is not 4818-M because that is for four-barrel carburetor cars. It is not 4816-F because that is applicable only to 360 V-8 two-barrels on Charger and Monaco. The correct number is 4816-G.

Of course, the catalog listings may be more specific, in which case you would not have to deduce the correct number.

Rebuilt parts. Rebuilding is an accepted aspect of automotive parts salvage, but when it comes to ignition parts, and most commonly spark plugs, you should avoid the rebuilt. It will not last as long as a new spark plug and often will not perform as well from the beginning.

7 | Doing the Tune-up

A tune-up entails more than merely installing new parts; it means installing the parts and adjusting them to specifications. Therefore, to do a successful tune-up on your car, you must know (1) the correct specification for each part; (2) how to make the adjustment; (3) how to check the adjustment against the specification. In this chapter you will learn how to remove the old part, install the new one, and adjust it according to specification.

The first step is to determine the correct specifications for:

Spark plug gap. This is the gap between the center and side electrodes, measured in thousandths of an inch or in millimeters. The specification will usually be written as .035″, which means thirty-five thousandths of an inch, or in metric terminology, something on the order of 0.8 mm, which is eight-tenths of a millimeter (roughly .032″).

Breaker-point gap. This is the gap between the contact faces of the points, and is also referred to as ignition-point gap or just point gap. As with spark-plug gap, it is given in thousandths of an inch or in millimeters. Usually an acceptable range is given, such as .013–.019″, which means that any gap between .013 and .019 inch is satisfactory.

Dwell angle. This is the time the breaker points are closed, measured in degrees. As with point gap, an acceptable range is given, such as 47–53°.

Ignition timing. The specification tells when the spark should occur and under what conditions. The terms BTDC (Before Top Dead Center), TDC (Top Dead Center), and ATDC (After Top Dead Center) will appear in the specification. The term Top Dead Center refers to the position of the piston in the cylinder. If it is at the very top of its stroke, it is said to be at TDC. Any time before it reaches the top it is BTDC and any time after it is ATDC. Although in theory the spark should occur at the plug when the piston is at the very top of its stroke and the fuel mixture is compressed to the maximum, actually a particular engine may perform better (either develop more power or lower exhaust emissions) if the spark occurs just a bit before or a bit after TDC. A typical specification might read "5 BTDC" or "5 ATDC"; to avoid error, you must see how the timing indicator is marked. Examples are given in this chapter. The timing indicator typically will have a zero (TDC) and degree markings on both sides (BDC and ATDC). Note the direction of engine rotation. The movable mark (on pulley or flywheel of the engine) passes the BTDC marks before it reaches the zero, the ATDC marks after passing zero.

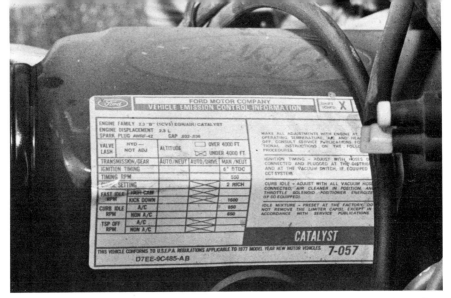

7-1. Late-model cars have a tune-up decal with some of the specifications you'll need.

Idle speed. The speed of an engine is given in revolutions per minute (rpm). Because most ignition timing specifications are based on readings with the engine idling, it is customary to check and adjust idle speed before performing the ignition timing check.

Compression. The compression developed by the piston in the cylinder is expressed in pounds per square inch (psi) or in metric terms as atmospheres, kilograms per square centimeter (kg/cm^2), or pascals.

WHERE TO GET SPECIFICATIONS. The specifications you need for automotive tune-up may be found in any of the following places:

Underhood decal. It may be on an underhood body panel or the engine top cover (Fig. 7-1). All late-model cars have such decals, but older cars do not. The decal may not list all tune-up specifications you need.

Factory service manual. The car manufacturer publishes a service manual for your car and it contains all service specifications. The owner's manual usually lists the price and address to which you should write for a copy.

General reference manual. A general reference manual is a digest of factory service manuals, generally covering a period of 6 to 10 years. Most good bookstores carry copies in their automotive book section.

Tune-up specification chart. Many manufacturers of automotive parts publish specification charts. Some auto parts stores will offer you a free copy if you buy the tune-up parts from them. Or if they don't have copies, they may have a general reference manual which you can inspect.

Public library. Most public libraries of reasonable size will have some types of automotive manuals with specifications. They may be factory service manuals, manufacturers' catalogs with tune-up specification charts or general reference manuals.

Once you have obtained tools, parts, and specifications, you're ready to begin.

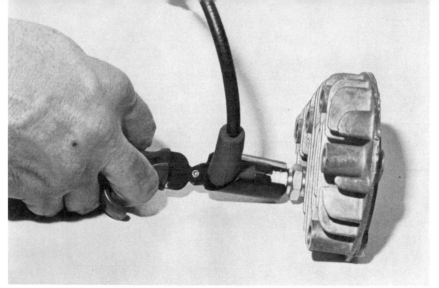

7-2. Special pliers grip the plug wire nipple firmly, enabling you to easily pull it off.

The jobs are listed in the sequence they should be done. The tune-up begins with spark-plug removal, is followed by compression testing, spark-plug installation, breaker-point replacement and adjustment, dwell test, air filter replacement, idle speed and ignition timing.

SPARK-PLUG REMOVAL. Always remove the spark plugs when the engine is warm but not hot. The reason: a compression test, which follows, is most accurate when the engine is warm or hot, but you're likely to burn yourself if you remove plugs from a hot engine.

Begin by disconnecting the plug wires from the spark plugs. There are special tools, many costing less than $2, for disconnecting wires that are not easily accessible (Fig. 7-2).

7-3. Wrong way to remove a plug wire. The wire is nonmetallic and may separate internally, causing a misfire.

7-4. Right way to handle a plug wire, by the nipple.

7-5. When the spark plug is reasonably accessible, as here, a ratchet and a short extension are all you need to remove it.

7-6. When there is an obstruction (in this car the back of the alternator), use a long extension to get above it.

If you can reach the plugs with your fingers, place them over the plug wire nipples, twist the nipples to break any heat seal, then pull straight out. Never pull on the plug wire itself, or you will cause it to break internally. See Fig. 7-3, 7-4. You'll never see the damage but the engine will misfire, perhaps not immediately but sooner than necessary.

As you disconnect each plug wire, wrap a piece of masking tape around it and write a number on it, starting from the front of the engine. Label the first plug No. 1, then 2, 3, etc., as you move rearward. This will prevent you from crossing the plug wires when you reconnect. Or you can obtain a synthetic rubber plug wire holder, already numbered.

When the plug wires are all disconnected, you're ready to remove the plugs. Select a deep socket of the appropriate size (13/16 or 5/8 inch) and determine what extensions (possibly a universal joint) are necessary. A little experimentation will be required the first time.

If the plug is just a short distance from an obstruction, such as an airconditioning compressor, alternator, or some rigid piping that is not easy to disconnect and move away, put the socket on the plug. Then try a very short extension and the ratchet (Fig. 7-5). If the ratchet butts up against the obstruction, remove the short extension and try putting the ratchet directly into the socket. If the ratchet handle now fouls against the engine and can't be turned in any position, perhaps a much longer extension rod will clear the obstruction (Fig. 7-6).

If not, put the universal joint on the socket and ratchet and see if that gives you an angle that permits turning the ratchet handle. You don't want to operate the universal joint at a severe angle, for that makes the ratchet difficult to handle, but often only a small angle is all you need to clear an obstruction.

7-7. The spark plug is really buried by air conditioning on this car. It looks impossible, but a ratchet with a curved handle and universal joint actually got the plug out easily.

Sometimes a spark-plug ratchet (Fig. 7-7) will permit you to slip into very tight quarters, and because it has a universal joint built into the head, you can tilt the handle away from the engine just enough to be able to swing it.

Set the ratchet to the "unthread" or "loosen" position. Every ratchet locks in one direction and turns freely in the other. If you want to remove a plug, set the ratchet so it locks when you try to pull the handle counterclockwise.

Make sure the socket is seated squarely on the plug. It should not wobble if it is in proper position. Most spark-plug sockets have a sponge rubber insert to hold the plug, so you may have to push down on the socket to seat it properly.

Place one hand on the head of the ratchet to brace it, then pull the handle with steadily increasing force. The plug should gradually loosen. If it doesn't, whack the end of the handle with the palm of your hand.

It is not uncommon for the socket to lift up and cock, particularly if a universal joint is being used and the ratchet is therefore at an angle. The plug's ceramic shell may crack or even break completely. Don't panic. Just reseat the socket on the hex, and with the ratchet remove the remains of the plug. With just minimal care, no pieces of ceramic will get into the spark-plug hole. You're discarding the old spark plug anyway, so who cares if it's cracked or broken?

When you have all the spark plugs out, inspect them for any signs of unusual problems. Photos of what you may see are shown in Figs. 7-8 to 7-11, along with the necessary remedies.

Note: If the plug was difficult to unthread, inspect the threads. If they contain gooey or hard deposits, clean the hole with the special tool available for the job.

With a magnet, determine if the area around the plug holes is cast iron or aluminum (nonmagnetic). If aluminum, the gooey deposits you may find are probably an anti-seize compound, designed to protect the aluminum from damage that could result if a spark plug seized in place. Spark plug threads should always be coated with a film of fresh anti-seize compound (available in auto parts stores serving the professional mechanic) before installation.

7-8. This spark plug is simply worn out. Notice the erosion of the electrodes. In fact, the center one is almost invisible.

7-9. This spark plug is oil-fouled. Possible causes: worn valve guides or piston rings. Have a mechanic test the engine.

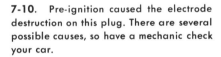

7-10. Pre-ignition caused the electrode destruction on this plug. There are several possible causes, so have a mechanic check your car.

7-11. This spark plug is fouled by carbon from the gasoline. It may be the wrong plug for the engine.

7-12. If you are using this type of compression gauge, hold it forcefully in the spark plug hole while the engine is being cranked, in order to get accurate readings.

COMPRESSION TEST. When all the spark plugs are out, you are ready to perform a compression test. Have a helper hold the gas pedal to the floor. If you are using the compression gauge shown in Fig. 7-12, you will have to hold it forcefully in the hole. If you have a gauge with a hose you can thread the hose into the hole.

Crank the engine for a few seconds. Read the gauge and write down the number. Depress the pressure-relief valve on the gauge (location varies with manufacturer; check instructions furnished with your tool), which will return the needle to zero. You're now ready to test another cylinder. Repeat the basic procedure for all cylinders.

All readings should be at least 90 pounds per square inch or greater (preferably 100 psi or more) and the difference between the lowest and highest reading should be no more than 30 percent. That is, if the highest reading is 150 psi, the lowest reading should be no less than 105 psi.

If you get an unusually low reading in one cylinder, repeat the test; you might not have held the gauge in properly.

If the differences between low and high readings are clearly greater than 30 percent, the engine will probably not run very smoothly, even if a complete tune-up is performed. You have a mechanical problem that must first be corrected.

GAPPING THE SPARK PLUGS. Remove the new spark plugs from their boxes and proceed to prepare them. If the top of the plug is threaded, and a cap is supplied, thread the cap onto the plug and tighten it with a pair of pliers.

Most spark plugs are gapped at the factory, but you still must check the gaps before you install them, for two reasons: (1) the factory-set gap may have changed as the plug was jostled in shipping; (2) the factory-set gap is usually for the most popular usage of the plug; this may not be the gap specified for your engine.

Insert the specified wire gauge between the electrodes (Fig. 7-13); it should go in and out with light-to-moderate drag. If the gauge won't fit in, or if it goes in and out very easily, the gap must be adjusted. Using the bracket on the plug gauge, bend the side electrode up or down to increase or decrease the gap (Fig. 7-14).

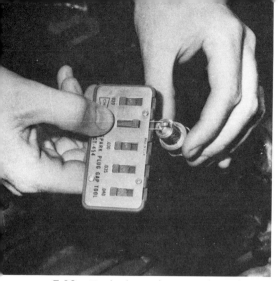

7-13. To check gap between electrodes, insert specified wire gauge. It should go in and out with light-to-moderate drag.

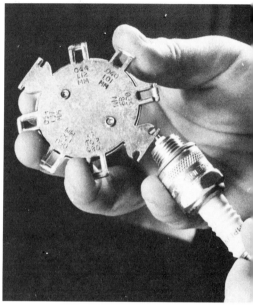

7-14. The bending bracket on a plug gauge is used to raise or lower the side electrode. This gauge is for spark plugs in electronic ignition systems.

When the gap is right, thread the plug into the hole by hand, being careful not to knock the tip against the engine. If you do slip, withdraw the plug and recheck the gap, for you may have knocked the side electrode closer to the center electrode, and reduced the gap.

Depending on the angle of installation, the plug may refuse to thread in. Don't force it; you may damage the threads on the plug and the cylinder head. Just keep trying, holding the plug by the hex section. If you find yourself ready to apply force, stop and take a break. Then try the plug in another hole, perhaps one you can see. The important thing is to avoid doing anything wrong from a sense of frustration. Difficulty in starting a spark plug is something that regularly afflicts professional mechanics, so bear in mind that you aren't the first person to encounter the problem.

If access to the plug hole is so poor you can't start the plug by hand, there are two techniques that may help you. Get a 4- to 6-inch piece of fuel line hose. Fit one end onto a Phillips screwdriver and the other onto the spark plug.

Hold the screwdriver by the handle and the hose will serve as a flexible shank to permit threading in the plug at an angle. An old spark-plug wire fitted onto the plug also can be used in a similar manner. If necessary, cut it short at the distributor cap end to make it easier to handle.

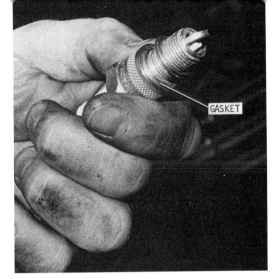

7-15. Spark plug with a gasket requires greater tightening than one without.

When the plug is threaded and hand-tightened, put on the socket and ratchet and tighten the plug. If the plug has a gasket (Fig. 7-15), a 90- to 180-degree turn of the handle will secure it. If it doesn't have a gasket, it is designed to wedge into place with just a slight nudge on the handle—a 20-degree turn at most. Don't overtighten. Very few spark plugs given any reasonable amount of tightening will loosen up, but overtightening may damage the threads, and at the least make the plug very difficult to remove a year or so later.

Before you push the plug wire back on, check its fit on an old spark plug from the same engine. If you can feel any looseness in the terminal when it is fitted to the spark plug, perhaps you can tighten up the terminal for a better fit, which may prevent misfire. If the terminal is straight, carefully push back the nipple to expose the metal part of the terminal, then gently squeeze together with slip-joint pliers (Fig. 7-16). If the plug wire ends in a right angle, wrap the nipple in a few layers of masking tape to protect it, then tighten the terminal with the pliers around the nipple.

7-16. If the plug wire terminal fits loosely on the plug, push back the nipple and tighten with pliers.

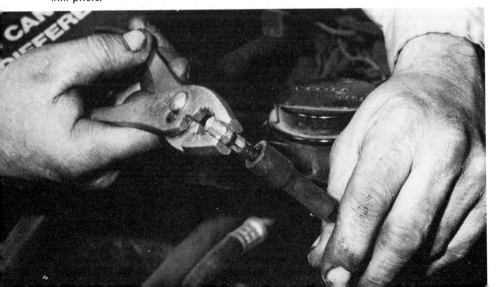

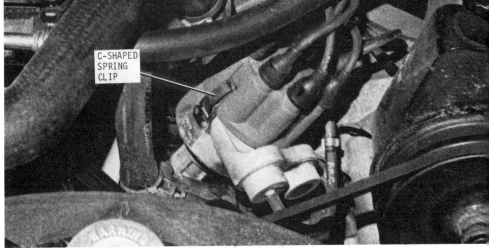

7-17. C-shaped spring clip is the most common type of clamp used to hold cap to the distributor body.

BREAKER POINTS. To gain access to the breaker points, remove the distributor cap, which is held either by C-shaped spring clips that fit onto the cap, by L-shaped, spring-loaded locking rods, or by screws.

To remove a cap held by spring clips (Fig. 7-17), just pry them off the cap with a screwdriver (Fig. 7-18). To reinstall, seat the cap properly (there are little notches in the body of the distributor and the cap for proper positioning), then push the curved section of the spring until the end of the spring arches onto the cap.

To remove a cap held by L-shaped rods (late-model General Motors cars), insert a Phillips screwdriver into the slot in the top of the rod, press down on the rod to compress the spring, then twist counterclockwise (Fig. 7-19). The bottom crossbar of the rod will be turned out from its holding position under the distributor body. When all rods are free (two or four, depending on the distributor) lift up the cap.

7-18. Insert screwdriver as shown to pry spring off retaining step on cap.

7-19. Many caps have L-shaped locking rods. Press down with screwdriver and turn counterclockwise.

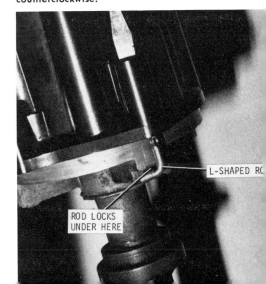

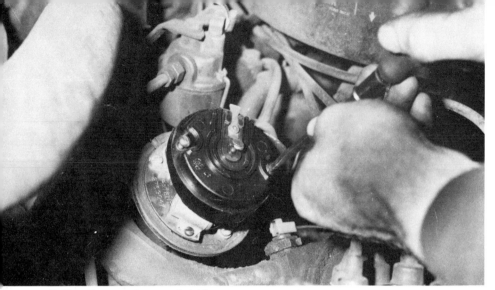

7-20. This round rotor is held by screws; remove them and lift it off.

To reinstall the cap, hold it down with one hand, then press the screwdriver into the top of each locking rod, compressing the spring and twisting the rod clockwise. Release the screwdriver and the spring will expand to lock the rod into place.

If the cap is held by screws, just unthread them until they are loose (they don't come out), then lift the cap free.

Removing the rotor. On most cars you can gain access to the points after removing the rotor. If it is held by screws remove them and lift it off. If not, pull it straight off (Figs. 7-21, 7-22). Some effort is necessary; the rotor will not just slide off.

On many late-model General Motors cars prior to 1975 (when the company began installing electronic ignition), there is a two-piece radio suppression shield around the points. It does not block access to the points' adjuster, but you have to remove it to replace the points. Take out the retaining screws and lift it off.

7-21. A screw-down retainer for distributor wiring is a common arrangement.

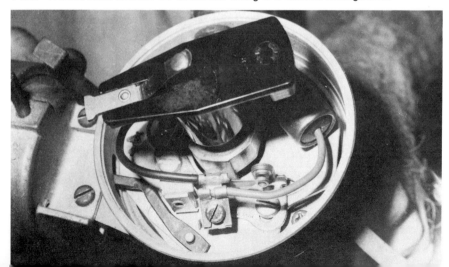

7-22. Removing screw that holds the fixed point.

Changing the points. Once you have access to the points, you will notice that one of them is fixed (held by a screw or two) and one of them is on a pivot and has a little block that bears against a shaft. Let's review their operation once again. The shaft is called the distributor cam and it contains several lobes. The cam is spun by the engine and each time a lobe bears against the block, it pushes the movable point away from the fixed point. As the distributor cam continues to turn, the lobe passes the block and the movable point springs back, into contact with the fixed point. This is how the points make and break an electrical circuit automatically.

To remove points, first disconnect the wires from the movable point. The method varies, but these are the most common attachments:

• Screw holds the wire terminals (Fig. 7-22).
• Wire has a spade connector that plugs in. Just pull it out.
• Nut holds wire terminals. Slacken nut and lift terminal up and out.

Next, with a magnetic screwdriver, remove the screw(s) that hold the fixed point (Fig. 7-22). On some Ford products a second screw also holds a wire from the plate on which the points mount. This wire is an electrical ground and should be handled tenderly (Fig. 7-23). On some cars the fixed point is held by a screw and the movable one by a clip that secures it to a pivot post on the breaker plate (Fig. 7-24). Finally, remove the screw that holds the condenser in place.

7-24. Sometimes a C-clip holds the movable point to the pivot post on the distributor breaker plate. Use two screwdrivers as shown to push the clip off.

7-23. On a Ford distributor a second screw holds the electrical ground wire.

GROUND CABLE

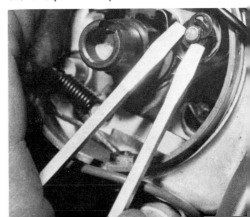

The screw(s) that hold the points are normally tight, so the screwdriver must fit the slot properly. When removing the screws be careful not to let them drop through any slots in the breaker plate. Retrieving them with a magnet could be very difficult.

When you have removed all the screws, lift the parts out of the distributor, noting how the points are positioned. You don't have to worry about the condenser or its connection if you install the combination breaker points and condenser set. You can treat the condenser as if it did not exist because it is completely integrated into the set of points.

Place the combination set into position and the holes for the retaining screw(s) will line up. Install them and tighten lightly on all but General Motors V-8 with the Peek-a-Boo distributor (see below).

Adjusting the points. You will notice that the retaining screw (on most sets) passes through an elongated hole in the fixed point plate (Fig. 7-25). The elongated hole is what permits the adjustment of the points, which consists of nothing more than precisely positioning the fixed point. (The movable point is pushed out the same distance every time by the lobes on the distributor cam, so the gap between the points is determined by the position of the fixed point.) Wherever in the elongated hole the screw is tightened, the fixed point stays. Here's how to make the adjustment:

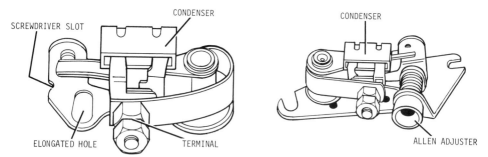

7-25. An elongated hole for the retaining screw and a screwdriver slot permit adjustment of breaker points in the combination set at left. If there is no elongated hole, there may be a separate adjuster, as in the General Motors set at right.

Short-burst-cranking method. The first step in points adjustment is to get the fiber block on the movable point pushed out to its maximum by a distributor cam lobe. One way this can be done is to crank the engine in very short bursts. (The engine won't start with the distributor cap off and the rotor removed, but for safety, disconnect the thick wire from the center of the coil.)

A short burst means that you turn the key to crank position and instantly release it. As the engine cranks, the distributor cam turns a little bit.

Of course, it is necessary to get the fiber block against the *peak* of a cam lobe (any one), not merely somewhere in contact with some part of the lobe. You will need a helper, either to look at the distributor or crank the engine for you.

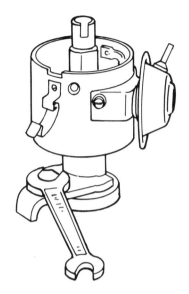

7-26. To turn the distributor body for points or timing adjustments, loosen the bolt at the base.

It may sound easy to line up the fiber block with the peak of the cam lobe by cranking the engine in short bursts, but you are likely to overshoot the position time after time.

If you're having trouble, here is a tip: When the fiber block is just short of the peak of a cam lobe, and you realize that another short burst of cranking will cause the lobe peak to overshoot, don't proceed to crank and waste effort. Instead, reinstall the rotor (as described later in this chapter) and, using it as a handle, turn the distributor cam. You'll find you can turn the cam a small fraction of an inch against spring pressure, and that small fraction may be enough to line up the fiber block and the peak of the cam lobe.

Have a helper hold the rotor in that perfect position and you can proceed to make a breaker points adjustment.

Note: Although this method is popular, you may find the following one, in which the distributor is loosened and turned, much easier. Many beginners are afraid of this technique, but what you will be doing is basically the same thing you must do to make an ignition timing adjustment. Inasmuch as ignition timing must be checked, and usually adjusted, following breaker points service, all you are doing is practicing a part of the procedure a few steps in advance.

Loosening-the-distributor method. Look at the very bottom of the distributor, where it meets the engine. You'll see a little bracket with a bolt holding the distributor in place (Fig. 7-26). Loosen that bolt with the proper wrench. With chalk or nail polish, make a mark on the base of the distributor and the engine directly next to it. This establishes the alignment of the distributor.

Now turn the distributor body clockwise or counterclockwise until the block of the movable point is on the peak of a distributor cam lobe. *Important:* If you have removed the bracket and locking bolt, or if the bracket has been turned, it is

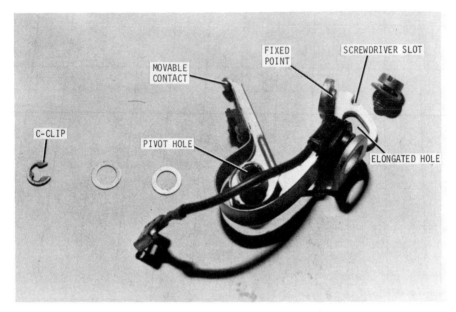

7-27.   This is the set of points removed from distributor shown in Fig. 7-24.

possible to lift the distributor out of the car. Don't! Once the distributor is removed from the car it requires special technique and care, in order to be able to reinsert it correctly. If you reinstall it wrong, the engine probably won't start. It may be tempting to lift the distributor out and work on it outside the car, where access to the points may be easier; however, even if you have to drape your body across the engine compartment to reach the distributor, this is what you should do, in order to replace points with the distributor remaining in place.

Once the block of the movable point in against the peak of a cam lobe, the movable point is pushed out as far as it will go when the engine is operating. The breaker point gap now can be adjusted.

Select a feeler gauge from your set that is equal to the specified breaker point gap. If a range is specified, such as .016–.020 inch, use the largest—in this case, .020 inch. This is because the gap decreases as the block on the movable point wears, so if you set the gap at the maximum, it will last longer. However, this is not critical, for the engine will operate satisfactorily even if the point gap closes a couple of thousandths of an inch below specifications.

On most fixed-point plates there is a little notch to accommodate a screwdriver (Fig. 7-27); once the screwdriver is in position, pushing it one way or the other will move the fixed point toward or away from the movable one. Lightly tightening the fixed-point retaining screw will provide some resistance to movement, just enough so the gap will hold at each position.

Begin by pushing the screwdriver until you see a gap between the movable and fixed points. Attempt to insert the feeler gauge (Figs. 7-28, 7-29). If, it won't fit in without pushing the movable point out still further, the gap is too small. If it will slide in and out very easily, the gap is too wide. The object is to get the gap so the gauge will go in and out with light to moderate drag. Once you have it, tighten the retaining screws securely.

7-28. Flat blade-type feeler gauge is inserted between conventional points to measure the gap.

7-29. A distributor with a combination set looks a bit empty without the separate condenser, but the points adjustment is still the same. Tighten retaining screw to secure the adjustment.

There are other types of point adjustments. The most common exception to the type described is the Peek-a-Boo used on GM cars with V-8 engines. The adjustment is made by turning an adjusting screw built into the points assembly (Fig. 7-30), using a 1/8-inch Allen wrench (Fig. 7-31). You can make a rough adjustment with the engine off. Line up the movable point block with the cam lobe, then turn the Allen wrench adjuster until you have a gap between fixed and movable points into which the feeler gauge will fit. The retaining screws for the breaker points can be tightened securely before adjustment.

7-30. GM V-8 distributor points are adjusted with an Allen wrench.

7-31. The Allen adjuster is accessible even with the radio suppression shield (used on some models) still in place.

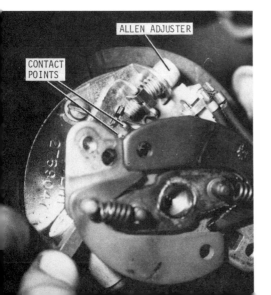

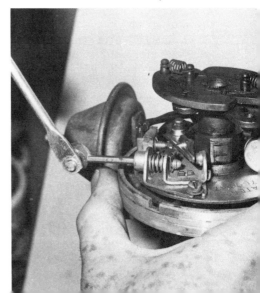

7-32. This is the Peek-a-Boo distributor cap with window up for points adjustment.

Final adjustment of the Peek-a-Boo design is with the engine running, using a dwellmeter. The distributor cap has a little metal window that you lift to gain access to the Allen wrench adjuster (hence the Peek-a-Boo nickname) as shown in Fig. 7-32.

On some foreign cars, the points are adjusted by turning an adjusting screw on the fixed-point plate. Turning the screw one way moves the fixed point to increase the gap, the other way to decrease it. If you see two screws on a foreign car fixed-point plate, check the design before you remove anything. Try to loosen both; if turning one of them changes the point gap, you've identified the design and the adjustment technique.

Finishing the job. Once the points are adjusted and the retaining screw(s) tight, move the distributor body back to realign the marks you made, then tighten the locking bolt.

Reconnect the wire to the breaker points and, on Ford products, the grounding wire to the retaining screw.

With a tiny brush, apply a film of grease to the distributor cam all around the area that comes in contact with the block on the movable point (Fig. 7-33). A vial of suitable grease is generally included with the points, or the points' set may have a lubricating wick attached, in which case no additional lubrication is necessary. If the points do not come with a grease vial, use silicone grease, commonly sold in tubes for lubrication around the home.

Look at the top of the distributor cam; if you see a piece of felt inside, it is a wick that should be lubricated. Squirt in a half-dozen drops of clean engine oil.

If there is a radio suppression shield, reinstall it, then the rotor. Make sure the notch on the push-on rotor is aligned with the slot in the distributor cam, then push on the rotor until it seats.

Reinstall the distributor cap and you're ready for the next step—a dwell test.

7-33. If points have no lubricating wick, apply white silicone grease to the area of the distributor cam that is in contact with the movable point.

DWELL. This is a term used to describe the time, in distributor degrees, during which the points are closed. Dwell is measured with a dwell-tachometer, an instrument that also measures engine rpm. If point gap is set correctly, dwell should also be correct. However, you must check to be sure, for the construction of the points is such that you might have to alter point gap somewhat (within its acceptable range) to also bring the dwell to within specifications.

To connect the dwell-tachometer, clip one wire to an electrical ground, such as an engine bolt; attach the other to one of the two thin-wire terminals on top of the coil, the one with the wire that goes to the breaker points. That terminal will be labeled with a minus sign (Fig. 7-34), CB or SW (for contact breaker or switch).

7-34. Dwell-tachometer is connected to the electrical ground and to the negative terminal of the coil, marked with a minus sign, "CB," or "SW."

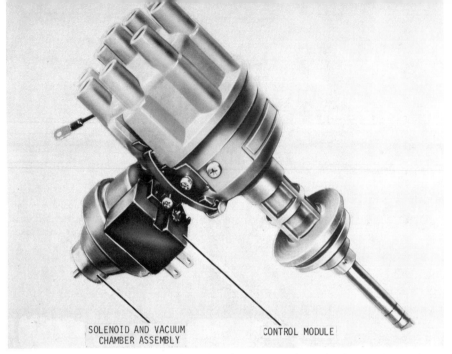

SOLENOID AND VACUUM
CHAMBER ASSEMBLY   CONTROL MODULE

7-35. If you have a pre-1973 Chrysler with a vacuum-control unit that has an electrical connector, remove the connector when making a dwell check.

Note: On Ford and Chrysler cars, disconnect and plug any hoses to the distributor. Also, on Chrysler cars, look for an electrical connector to the part of the distributor where the hoses attach (see Fig. 7-35). Remove that connector for the
dwell test, on cars so equipped.

Start the engine and let it idle. Turn the switch on the dwell-tachometer to
dwell and the cylinder selector to the number of cylinders of the engine. The
reading on the degrees dial is the dwell, and it should be within specifications.
Anywhere in the range specified is acceptable.

If the dwell reading is too low, the point gap is too great. If the dwell reading is
too high, the point gap is too small. Even if the point gap is within specifications,
it should be possible to adjust it to get both point gap and dwell within specifications.

On GM V-8 engines, lift the window on the cap, insert an 1/8-inch Allen
wrench and turn it as necessary to get the dwell within specifications. Don't
worry about the breaker points' gap on this one.

You can also check your distributor with a dwell-tachometer. Turn the switch
to get an engine speed reading, have a helper step on the gas pedal to raise
engine speed to 1500 and 2000 rpm—and hold it there. Then switch back to
dwell. The reading should be within three degrees of the original reading. If not,
the distributor is worn. If you encounter performance problems, a replacement
distributor may be necessary. Some engines will perform acceptably with dwell
variations greater than normal; others will not.

AIR FILTER REPLACEMENT. On most cars air filter replacement is a simple
matter of removing a wingnut and lifting the air filter housing cover (Fig. 7-36),
then lifting the circular filter element up and out and installing a replacement
(Fig. 7-37). Refit the cover, tighten the wingnut and you're done.

92

7-36. To get at the air filter, remove the wingnut that holds the cover in place.

7-37. Lift the cover and take out the old element, then install a new one.

On cars with sealed filters, such as Chevrolet Vega and Chevette, the entire cannister is replaced, which means a hose or two must be disconnected, as shown in Fig. 7-38.

7-38. On cars with sealed cannister air filters, a major section of the air filter housing is discarded. Disconnect hose when removing the cannister, as shown.

On foreign cars, the filter housing cover may be held with spring clips or nuts, but the removal procedure will be obvious. One of the few cars that may pose difficulty is the VW Rabbit with fuel injection. On this model only, the fuel distributor is mounted on the air cleaner housing cover, which is held with spring clips. After you slacken the spring clips you may or may not be able to lift the cover sufficiently to remove the filter. If necessary, follow the fuel line from the fuel distributor to the nearest connection point, loosen the line there, and wrap a rag around the connection to catch any fuel drippage. Now you can lift the cover and withdraw the filter. After reinstalling or replacing the filter, remember to tighten the fuel line connection.

SETTING IDLE SPEED. Let the engine warm up, switch the test meter from dwell to tach, and take an engine idle speed reading, which is the speed the engine runs at with no pressure on the gas pedal. If it is within specifications, proceed to ignition timing. If not, it must be adjusted.

The adjustment procedure varies widely according to specific models, engines, and carburetors. There are six completely different arrangements in common use, and you must look at the carburetor to determine which one is used on your car. In order to get a close look, you must remove the entire air cleaner housing, so let's begin with that.

Remove the wingnut or whatever clip holds the cover. You should then be able to lift the housing. *Note:* On some cars there will be a flexible duct attached to the housing. Undo the clip and pull that off.

Once you lift the housing up, you can see all the hoses attached to it. Make a simple sketch of the hose connections. To be extra sure, apply masking tape to each hose and its connection point on the air cleaner housing and label the tape with a marking pen. The hoses normally are not held by clamps, so you can just twist and pull them off.

With the air cleaner out of the way, look at the carburetor while a helper presses and releases the gas pedal. You will see linkage on the carburetor move in response to operation of the gas pedal. That is the throttle linkage. The plate it controls in the carburetor is the throttle, and it controls engine speed.

Here are some of the specific things you may note at the carburetor throttle linkage.

1. The linkage has a tab that bears against a screw when the gas pedal is completely released. In the absence of any of the following items, that is the idle speed adjusting screw. If you turn it in, it prevents the throttle linkage from closing, which is the same as stepping lightly on the gas pedal—engine speed goes up. If you unthread the screw, the throttle can close farther, equivalent to releasing the gas pedal even further than it normally goes. Idle speed is reduced.

2. There are two screws that bear against the throttle linkage (Fig. 7-39). One is for idle speed, the other is for fast idle, a higher-than-normal idle speed for when the engine is cold. The fast idle screw is the one that bears against a curved, stepped tab that you can move back and forth when the engine is warm. The single screw in the first example may bear against such a curved tab—called a fast idle cam—but that one screw does double duty, handling both fast and normal idle speed.

3. There is a solenoid that bears against the throttle linkage. A solenoid is an electromagnetic switch that you can identify by its plunger and an electrical connector (see Fig. 7-4 for one example). The solenoid is activated when the ignition

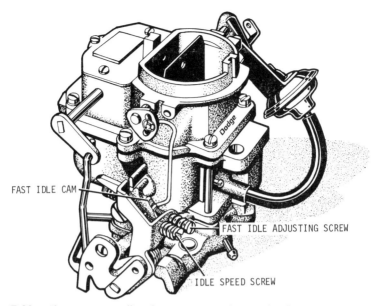

FAST IDLE CAM

FAST IDLE ADJUSTING SCREW

IDLE SPEED SCREW

7-39. Shown are two idle adjusting screws. The one that bears against the fast idle cam is for fast idle only. Use the idle speed screw for normal adjustments. If the carburetor has only one screw, the idle speed is set with it on the lowest point of the cam (at which it will be if the idle speed is set with engine warmed up, as specified).

is turned on, and it ejects the plunger to bear against the throttle linkage. The purpose: to hold the throttle linkage open and maintain idle speed. When the ignition is turned off, a spring retracts the plunger, permitting the throttle to close more completely. The engine shuts off positively, to prevent afterrun. If you have a late-model car without a solenoid, you may have experienced afterrun, also called dieseling, in which the engine continues to run for several seconds after you've turned the key.

If the carburetor has a solenoid, it probably is involved in the idle speed adjustment. To find out, watch the plunger as a helper first holds the gas pedal down and then turns on the ignition. If the plunger extends, the solenoid is involved. Look for one of the following solenoid designs:

• Adjustable plunger. If the tip of the plunger is square or hex shaped, the idle speed is set by turning the plunger in or out with a wrench on the plunger tip, as shown in Fig. 7-40.

• Adjustable carriage. If the solenoid is on an adjustable carriage, as in Fig. 7-41, turn the big screw, to move the solenoid toward or away from the throttle linkage.

• Solenoid plunger bears against adjusting screw on throttle linkage. To adjust idle speed, turn the screw. This is similar to making an adjustment on a carburetor without a solenoid.

• Entire solenoid body is adjustable. In this design the entire solenoid body is like a big adjusting screw, and there is a hex on the back of the body to permit turning it with a wrench (Fig. 7-42). There also is a hole in the back of the solenoid (it goes through the middle of the hex section), into which an Allen wrench is inserted to turn a second adjuster inside the solenoid (see Fig. 7-43).

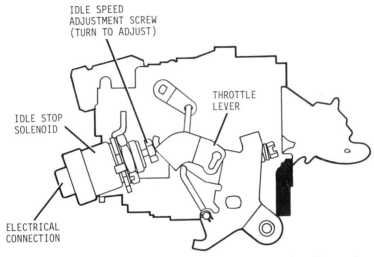

7-40. This solenoid has an adjustable plunger for setting the idle speed.

7-41. To reposition adjustable carriage on this solenoid design, turn the screw as shown.

7-42. Hex on back of this solenoid body is turned to make basic idle speed adjustment. Note the hole in center of the hex, which is for the Allen wrench.

7-43. To fine tune the idle speed setting, Allen wrench is inserted into back of solenoid.

• There is an adjusting rod with a square or hex end projecting from the back of the solenoid. Just turn the rod to adjust idle speed.

With the dwell-tachometer connected, and the engine warmed up and idling, you must be able to reach the idle speed adjustment, whether it be a screw or on a solenoid. It also is important that all hoses going to the carburetor be connected, although the air cleaner housing itself may have to be lifted partly to be able to reach the adjuster.

To increase idle speed, turn the screw, solenoid body, or adjusting rod on back of solenoid clockwise. On other arrangements you will have to turn the adjuster both ways to find out which increases and which decreases idle speed.

To reduce idle speed, reverse the adjustment.

On those cars in which the entire solenoid body is turned by the hex on the back, begin by turning the internal Allen adjuster clockwise until it seats and no longer will move. Then turn the entire solenoid body with a wrench on the hex, to get an idle speed 150 rpm above specifications. Finally, turn the internal Allen adjuster counterclockwise (back it out) to the specified idle speed.

Adjustment techniques. The solenoid plunger is not pushed out forcefully enough to actually change the idle speed. If the throttle is opened, however, it will extend and hold its new position. Therefore, whenever you make an adjustment that involves the solenoid, always blip the throttle. (Have a helper hit the gas pedal or manually operate the throttle linkage from under the hood, as shown in Fig. 7-44.)

All idle speed specifications are accurate if plus or minus 50 rpm. If the specification is 850 rpm, therefore, anywhere between 800 and 900 rpm is satisfactory.

Be sure to note that idle speed is set in Neutral on manual transmission cars, in Drive with the parking brake firmly applied on automatics, unless the underhood tune-up decal says otherwise.

7-44. Move linkage at carburetor to "blip" the throttle. This will extend the solenoid plunger far enough to hold the idle speed adjustment.

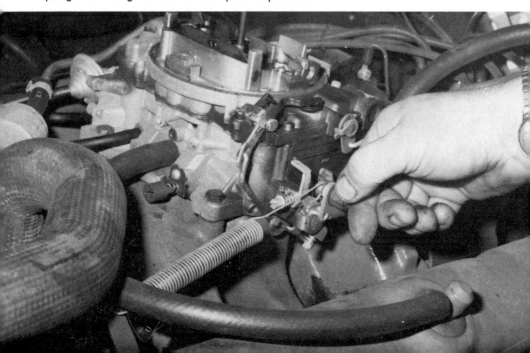

IGNITION TIMING. With idle speed set to specifications, breaker point gap and dwell correct (on cars without electronic ignition) you're ready to check ignition timing—that is, the timing of the firing of the spark plug. To do this, you connect the timing light to the battery and to No. 1 spark plug or its wire (depending on the design of the timing light). Then you start the engine and aim the light at the timing marks, the location of which we will explain shortly. Every time the No. 1 spark plug fires, the light will go on, and you will be able to see the timing marks. They should be aligned. If they are not, you must adjust the distributor to bring the marks into alignment.

To be able to connect the light to No. 1 plug and its wire, you must know which is No. 1, and each car maker has a different numbering system, which does not appear anywhere near the plugs nor, in most cases, anywhere on the car. Here is a guide to cylinder numbering.

American cars with in-line engines (cylinders one behind the other): No. 1 is the first spark plug from the front of the car.

American cars with V-6 or V-8 engines (except Fords and *full-size* Cadillacs): No. 1 is on the driver's side at the very front.

Ford cars and full-size Cadillacs: No. 1 is at the very front on the passenger's side of the car.

Volkswagen air-cooled engines: No. 1 is on the passenger's side and is the forward spark plug (not the one closest to the rear bumper).

Volkswagen Rabbit and Scirocco: No. 1 is the first spark plug, counting from the passenger's side of the car.

Foreign cars with in-line engines (except Jaguar): No. 1 is the first spark plug, counting from the front of the engine. On the Jaguar 6-cylinder it is the first spark plug counting from the rear of the engine.

Timing Marks. Next, locate the timing marks. On all American cars there is a mark or dial on the crankshaft pulley assembly at the very front of the engine, and a stationary pointer or dial on a front sheet-metal cover of the engine.

On most foreign cars, the marks are in the same place. A significant exception is Volkswagen.

On the air-cooled engine (Beetle, etc.) there is a notch on the crankshaft pulley and a vertical joint where the two halves of the engine are bolted together which serves as the stationary indicator (Fig. 7-45).

On water-cooled VW engines, the mark is on the flywheel, visible through a hole in the flywheel housing, a metal structure bolted to the rear of the engine. See Fig. 7-46. A similar mark location is used for some Toyota models.

Even with a good timing light, the marks may not be readily visible if you don't make special preparations. If the marks are covered with road film, wipe them clean (Fig. 7-47). A pulley notch may not be particularly visible unless you apply bright nail polish or chalk to it.

Vacuum lines. There are one or two hoses connected to the exterior of the distributor. These hoses are vacuum lines. They are attached to a diaphragm device on the distributor called a vacuum control unit. The vacuum unit measures engine vacuum and adjusts ignition timing in accordance with it. The vacuum developed by an engine is an indication of the load it is under, and ignition timing is varied automatically, according to changes in load, by the vacuum control unit.

7-45. Finger points to center joint of crankcase halves on VW Beetle engine. That center joint is the fixed reference for timing adjustments. Crankshaft pulley may have as many as three notches; check specifications to be sure which one to use on your model car.

7-46. Timing mark on water-cooled Volkswagens is on the flywheel. To gain access, remove threaded plug with electrical connector. Timing is checked by aiming the light at the hole. The number 3 should be illuminated when the timing light goes on.

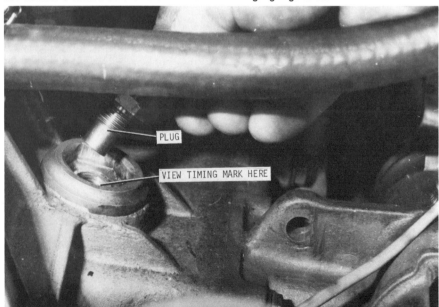

PLUG

VIEW TIMING MARK HERE

7-47. If timing marks are dirty, clean them with a cloth.

The diaphragm in the vacuum control unit is connected by a link to the plate on which the breaker points are mounted. Vacuum causes the diaphragm to flex and this pulls on the link and moves the plate. If the plate pivots one way, the points open earlier and ignition occurs earlier. When the diaphragm relaxes, a spring retracts everything, the plate returns to its normal position, and ignition is retarded. On some cars there are two diaphragms, one of which is designed to retard timing under certain conditions, to reduce exhaust emissions.

The ignition timing specified by the car maker is called basic timing. This means it doesn't include any contribution made by the vacuum control unit, or a mechanical speed-sensitive unit built into the distributor.

Setting ignition timing at idle means that engine speed is sufficiently low so that mechanical advance is not really functional. To eliminate the vacuum control from the picture too, the hoses at the distributor are disconnected and plugged, with a golf tee, pencil, or other suitable device (Fig. 7-48).

7-48. Before checking ignition timing, disconnect hose from distributor and plug it with a pencil or golf tee.

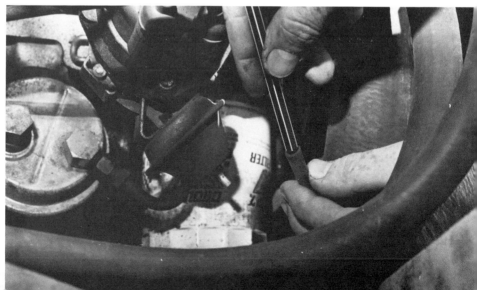

7-49. To avoid a distorted reading, get a straight-on view of timing marks from just above the timing light.

Note: On a few cars, primarily imports, the ignition timing is not checked at idle speed, and in a rare case, the car maker may specify that the check be made with the vacuum hose(s) connected. If that's what the specifications call for, that's what you must do. The ignition timing number given by the car maker compensates for the fact that engine speed is above idle, and/or the vacuum hose(s) is connected.

If you must check timing at a speed above idle, connect the tachometer and turn the idle speed adjuster until it reads the rpm number specified. Turn it back to specifications after timing is correct.

Taking the reading. Aim the timing light at the marks from a straightaway position, not an angle, and view them from just above the top of the timing light (see Fig. 7-49). This will give you the most accurate reading. If the light hits the marks from an angle, and you also look at the marks from the same angle, you get a distorted view.

On some cars the timing marks are in such a poor location, obstructed by engine compartment accessories, that it is impossible to both aim and look from a straightaway position. On such cars the timing indicator on the front of the engine has a hole that holds a magnetic probe (Fig. 7-50), and a special timing indicator is used, so the mechanic does not actually have to see the marks. Unfortunately, this special equipment costs about $300, so it is obviously out of the question for the weekend mechanic. But you have another choice: making a second set of timing marks in a more convenient location.

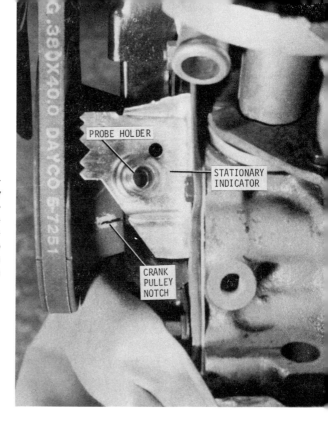

7-50. When timing mark is hidden from view, the indicator may have a probe holder. An electromagnetic probe can be inserted into this holder and trigger a digital timing device to which it is wired. The ignition timing, in degrees, is shown on the device.

To make a second set of marks, find an alternate location with the car up on safety stands or ramps. Line up the mark on the pulley and the stationary indicator by hand. This should be done with the spark plugs out, so the engine can be turned more easily. Squeeze the alternator drive belt together at opposite points a few inches away from the pulley, and simultaneously pull the top end of the belt, turning the engine until the marks line up. This is not easy, but you can reduce the distance necessary by cranking the engine in short bursts until the marks are virtually aligned. Then you have only to make the alignment precise.

Note: If you have not removed the spark plugs, disconnect the thick wire from the center of the coil (or at its other connection point, the center of the distributor cap) so the engine won't start. On GM cars with electronic ignition, squeeze the tab and remove the terminal with the thin pink wire from the distributor (Fig. 7-51).

Make new marks in the accessible location with a file (Fig. 7-52) or with a wire pointer attached to a nearby bolt (Fig. 7-53).

If the wire leads from your timing light do not permit the light to reach the battery and No. 1 spark-plug wire from your viewing point, obtain jumper wires of suitable length and connect them to the clips of the timing light's wires. Tape over the connections between timing light wires and jumper wires, to prevent a short circuit.

Now turn on the engine, let it warm up and idle, aim the light at the marks, pull the trigger, and see that the marks are precisely aligned. If the mark on the pulley does not align with the stationary mark, you must make an adjustment. Just loosen the bolt or nut that holds the distributor at its base (the same one you loosened in order to move the distributor for breaker-point adjustment). Turn the distributor body—clockwise or counterclockwise—in whichever direction will bring the correct marks into alignment. Remember, although the pulley or stationary indicator may have a number of marks, only one is specified for your engine. Alignment with another mark on the indicator is not good enough. Only a very small movement of the distributor should align the marks, so turn the distributor very slowly.

When timing is correct, tighten the distributor lock bolt or nut, then unplug and reconnect the hose(s) to the vacuum control unit.

7-51. On GM cars with electronic ignition, there is a pink wire connected to the distributor with a tab. To prevent the car from starting, squeeze the tab and remove the terminal.

7-52. If you want to remark the engine, line up the timing marks, then make a new set elsewhere on the engine in a more convenient spot. Here a mark is being made on the pulley and on the oil pan lip, the stationary indicator.

7-53. Here a timing point was made from a piece of wire securely attached to an oil pan bolt, and braced against a lip on the oil pan. A notch was filed in the pulley.

8 | Major Tune-up

A "major tune-up" is as undefined a term as tune-up itself. If you want to do more to achieve easier starting and smoother operation, service the items covered in this chapter.

ELECTRONIC IGNITION. Although electronic ignition eliminates the breaker points and condenser, the system itself is not completely trouble-free.

Complete testing of the electronic ignition system requires skills and special equipment beyond the reach of the average weekend mechanic, but there are a couple of inspections you can make.

Remove the distributor cap and look at the trigger wheel and pickup coil sensor (Fig. 8-1). These are the parts that signal the transistorized circuit to trigger the coil. If the distributor is worn and they have vibrated into occasional contact with each other, you will see obvious damage on the edges of the trigger wheel. Have the problem corrected by a professional mechanic immediately.

If the parts look good physically, you can check the pickup coil, the part most likely to malfunction in an electronic ignition system. Look up the specification for pickup coil resistance; you can measure it with an ohmmeter. The resistance values vary from car to car; some are under 2 ohms, others close to 1000 ohms.

To make the check you must find the terminal for the two wires that come from the pickup coil. It should be obvious; on most cars they go to a connector somewhere near the distributor (Fig. 8-2). The exception is General Motors cars, on which they go to a tiny part inside the distributor (Figs. 8-3 and 8-4). That is the transistorized control unit that triggers the ignition coil.

Undo the connector from the pickup coil or, on GM cars, disconnect the two wires from the control unit. Connect an ohmmeter lead wire to each of the terminals of the two-wire connector. *Note:* On Ford products there may be three wires at the connector. Ignore the black wire, which is an electrical ground. If the ohmmeter reading is within specifications, the pickup coil passes the test. If above or below specifications, it must be replaced, a job that on most cars will have to be done by a professional mechanic.

Move one ohmmeter wire from one of the two terminals on the connector to any electrical ground, such as an engine bolt or the distributor body (or on Ford cars, the terminal for that black wire). The ohmmeter reading should be infinity, indicating the pickup coil is not electrically grounded. If you get any reading short of infinity, the part is grounded. Look first for a cut or worn-away piece of insulation on the wiring from the pickup coil. You may be able to tape over a break in the insulation and correct the problem, but if the wiring is good, the pickup coil must be replaced.

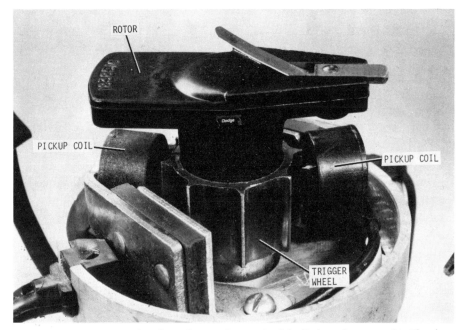

8-1. Electronic ignition distributor has a trigger wheel (called a reluctor on this Chrysler model) and a pickup coil.This distributor has two coils, part of a special design that includes electronic spark timing.

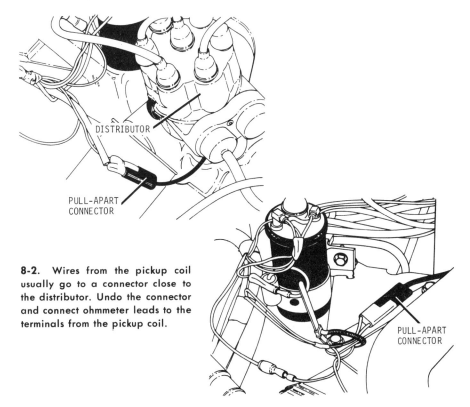

8-2. Wires from the pickup coil usually go to a connector close to the distributor. Undo the connector and connect ohmmeter leads to the terminals from the pickup coil.

WIRES FROM PICKUP COIL

TRANSISTORIZED
CONTROL UNIT

8-3. This is a General Motors electronic ignition distributor, in which the transistorized control unit is inside the distributor. To test the pickup coil, disconnect wires from the transistorized control unit.

8-4. Wires have been disconnected from the transistorized control unit. Ohmmeter leads can easily be connected to them to check the pickup coil.

SPARK-PLUG WIRES. The spark-plug wires used on the modern car are the resistance type—that is, they control the flow of electricity to the spark plugs in such a way as to minimize radio interference. In most cars they combine with resistor spark plugs, which also contribute to reduction in interference.

The resistance spark-plug wire is nonmetallic. It is a cloth fiber material impregnated with carbon to form the electrical conductor. You can't tell this by looking at the wire, because it's covered by a synthetic rubber insulating jacket. If the wire is carelessly handled, it separates internally and can cause the engine to misfire; hence the warnings about handling procedure in the previous chapter. The resistance values in the wire can change with age, and it is not uncommon for them to increase very substantially in just three to four years of car operation.

Here are two simple tests for spark-plug wires:

First, inspect them visually. If they are oil-soaked or heat-cracked, replace them. Next, if you have an ohmmeter, disconnect the wire at each end (it's not necessary to remove it from the engine) and touch or connect each ohmmeter lead to each metal terminal (Fig. 8-5). The reading should be no more than 15,000 ohms per foot of length of the spark-plug wire. If it is excessive, the wire should be replaced.

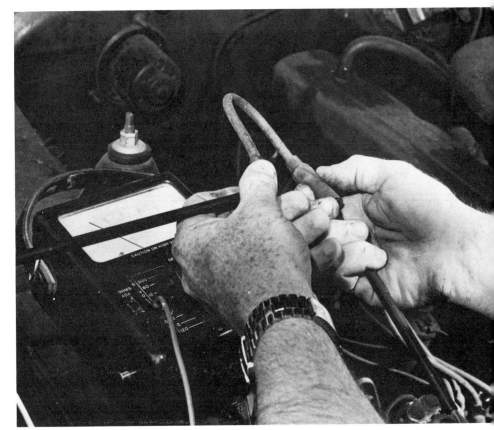

8-5.   Testing spark-plug wire with ohmmeter leads attached to each end of wire. Plug wire need not be removed from the engine for the test, just disconnected at each end.

8-6. Custom set of spark-plug wires has terminals factory-fitted to each end.

Replacing plug wires. If the spark-plug wires require replacement, you have several choices.

• You may be able to replace only the defective wires. On new cars, the wires may be very expensive because they are covered with super-premium insulation—silicone rubber. The price of a set of eight is $30 to $65, so individual wires at $4 to $10 have been placed on the market.

• You can get a universal set of spark-plug wires. These wires are long and have the terminal attached at the spark-plug end. You trim the other end (for the distributor cap) as required; then fit a protective nipple and, using pliers, attach a terminal.

• Custom set of plug wires (Fig. 8-6). The plug wires are complete in every respect and are within a couple of inches of the length of the original wires.

• A make-your-own set with a roll or pieces of wire, and terminals and protective nipples. You cut the wire, attach terminals and nipples to each end.

Clearly, the custom set is the most expensive, but it should be your choice, for these reasons:

Attaching terminals to plug wires with a pair of pliers does not give you as reliable a connection as an attachment made on a factory machine.

The make-your-own set is particularly vulnerable to problems if the wire is the nonmetallic resistance type, which has been used as original equipment for about twenty years. Making sure you have a good connection from a metal terminal to a nonmetallic electrical conductor can be tricky business.

The universal and make-your-own sets are not always resistance wire. If you use a metal-core wire, some parts of the ignition system might be adversely affected by the changes in the voltage.

The universal and make-your-own sets may not be readily available in premium silicone rubber insulation. Not all cars need silicone rubber, but late models, with their high underhood temperatures, should have the extra protection it provides. Silicone rubber also helps hold in high voltage found in many electronic ignition systems.

Custom sets are sold in either of the following materials:

Silicone rubber insulation with silicone nipples (usually at both ends, but at least at the spark-plug end where its resistance to heat deterioration is more critical. Most late-model cars have spark-plug wires that are 7 mm in diameter (.028 inch), but those with high-performance electronic ignition systems require even thicker silicone rubber insulation and are 8mm in diameter (.032 inch).

Hypalon with silicone or hypalon nipples. Hypalon is a synthetic rubber that is heat-resistant but not quite as good as silicone rubber. It is acceptable on pre-1971 cars and will survive on late models, particularly those without electronic ignition, although not as long as silicone rubber. If you are planning to keep your car for no more than three years, hypalon should do the job and provide a savings. This is true even with electronic ignition if a silicone rubber nipple is used at the hottest point—the spark plug. The difference in cost between hypalon with silicone nipples and hypalon/hypalon nipples is relatively small (usually under $2 per set of eight).

The only way to install new spark-plug wires is one at a time. This is the way a smart professional does it, too. You eliminate the danger of making incorrect connections, which would result in engine misfire, and you insure correct routing of the wires. If plug wires are not routed exactly as the car maker did, there is a danger they may come in contact with a hot engine part and be burned, or that two plug wires could crossfire (transfer current from one to the other) and cause misfire. Crossfire is only a problem on wires that are attached to plugs that fire consecutively, and the car maker's routing is designed to prevent it (see Fig. 8-7).

On most engines the method of disconnecting the plug wire at both ends is obvious—just grasp at the nipple, twist, and pull off. The exception is the General Motors High Energy Ignition System, which has been used since 1975. With this design you must first lift off a plastic cage that holds the wires in place on the distributor cap (Fig. 8-8).

Be careful to engage the wire in each little guide and holder that the car maker has installed. They are there to help insure correct routing.

8-7. Observe unusual spark-plug wire routing. It's designed to prevent crossfire, which causes engine to miss.

8-8. On GM electronic ignition, plug wires must be disconnected from plastic cage.

8-9. In-line gas filter is held by clamps on pieces of short hose in the line from the fuel pump to the carburetor. The type shown has spring clamps, so special pliers are used to move clamps for filter replacement.

GASOLINE FILTER. The carburetor of your engine needs clean fuel to function properly, for dirt in gasoline can affect many delicate internal parts of the carburetor. There is a coarse permanent filter in the gas tank, but the filter that really does the job is somewhere between the fuel pump and the carburetor. It is a very fine filter.

On most cars the fine filter is spliced into the fuel line itself with short pieces of rubber hose (Fig. 8-9) or inserted in the carburetor, at the point where the fuel line from the pump is connected (Fig. 8-10). On a few cars the filter is attached to the fuel pump (Fig. 8-11).

The filter should be replaced once a year, as part of a major tune-up. Here's how to do the job.

In-line filter. Remove the hose clamps or at least reposition them from the ends of the fuel line to the middle of the short pieces of hose. Next, disconnect the short hoses from the fuel line and remove them with the filter.

8-10. Little filter fits into the inlet section of the carburetor, at the point where fuel enters from the fuel line. Fuel line and the inlet fitting have been removed to get to the filter.

8-11. To replace the filter on the fuel pump (on some Ford cars), just unscrew the cover, then change the filter inside and hand-tighten the cover.

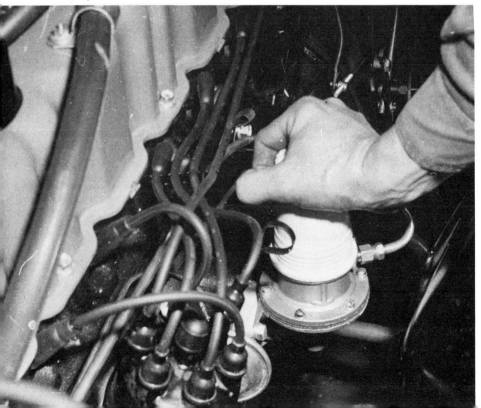

Attach the short pieces of hose to the necks of the new filter and secure them to the filter necks with whatever types of clamps are provided with the new filter (Fig. 8-12).

Observe the arrow on the filter assembly. The filter should be installed so that the arrow is pointing to the section of the fuel line that connects to the carburetor.

Place the remaining hose clamps on each section of fuel line, then install the filter by pushing the short hoses onto the sections of fuel line—at least 3/4 inch from the end of each piece of fuel line. Move the clamps from the fuel line sections into position over the hoses and, if they are not the spring type, tighten them.

Filter on pump. If the filter is on the fuel pump itself, unscrew the cover (Fig. 8-11). Remove the old filter and discard, then install the new one and refit the cover hand tight.

Filter in carburetor inlet. If the filter is in the carburetor inlet, you must disconnect the fuel line from the carburetor with a pair of open-end wrenches. One wrench is placed on the hex of the fitting that is part of the carburetor; the other is

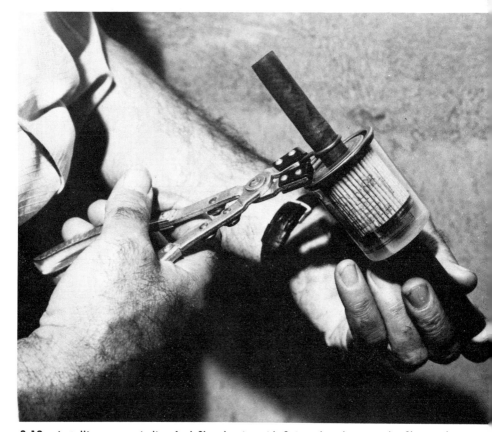

8-12.   Installing a new in-line fuel filter begins with fitting short hoses to the filter and securing them to filter necks with clamps.

placed on the hex nut that holds the line to the carburetor fitting (Fig. 8-13). Apply clockwise pressure with the wrench to the carburetor fitting while you exert counterclockwise pressure (to loosen) the fuel line nut. Once the nut is loose, unthread it all the way and catch any fuel drippings in a can. Finally, unthread the carburetor fitting itself, using the wrench that was holding it in place. As you remove the fitting, the filter will come out too (Fig. 8-10). A tiny spring also will come out.

Install a new filter and the spring. If the filter is a bronze cone instead of the conventional pleated paper, install it so the small end faces outward. Thread in the carburetor fitting (by hand) and tighten securely with the wrench. Then thread on the fuel line nut (also by hand) and tighten with the wrench. The purpose of starting the parts by hand is to prevent cross-threading, which would damage the threads and permit fuel leakage.

POSITIVE CRANKCASE VENTILATION. The crankcase of your engine is the portion that houses the crankshaft, and to which the oil reservoir—the pan—is attached. As the engine operates, some fuel mixture in the combustion chamber does not get burned—it slips past the pistons in the crankcase where it turns to fumes that circulate throughout many parts of the engine. On older cars these fumes were expelled into the atmosphere, where they contributed to air pollution. On all cars since 1963, they are recirculated back into the cylinders for buring.

8-13. If the fuel filter is at the carburetor inlet, remove the fuel line with two wrenches, one to hold carburetor inlet fitting, the other to loosen the fuel line nut. After the fuel line is off, use the wrench to remove the inlet fitting.

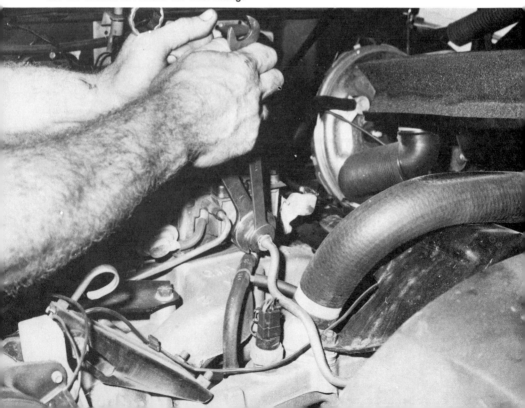

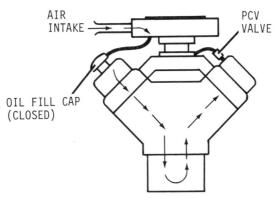

8-14. How the Positive Crankcase Ventilation system works. Air is drawn in through the fresh-air inlet, helping to purge crankcase fumes, which are drawn into the carburetor base by engine vacuum. PCV valve, a flow-control, regulates the flow of fumes according to what the engine can handle: minimum flow at idle, maximum flow when throttle is open.

This is accomplished by hoses and a flow-control valve, in a system called Positive Crankcase Ventilation (PCV for short). Vacuum developed in the cylinders sucks the fumes from other parts of the engine into the base of the carburetor, where they combine with fuel mixture. The combination is drawn into the cylinders and burned. The purging of these fumes is assisted by a supply of clean fresh air admitted to the engine.

Fig. 8-14 shows how the typical system works. Air is drawn from the air cleaner assembly through a tiny filter inside the housing. The air flows into the engine through the top cover, to the crankcase, and pushes away the fumes. The fumes are drawn up from the crankcase into the top of the engine, and from there into the PCV valve. This valve regulates the flow of fumes according to the vacuum developed in the engine. An engine develops less vacuum at high speed, more vacuum at low speed. When vacuum is low, indicating the engine is at high speed, the valve admits a maximum amount of fumes into the base of the carburetor. When vacuum is high, indicating the engine is at low speed, the valve reduces the flow of fumes.

The valve is necessary to control the flow of fumes, as they should compose only a limited portion of the fuel mixture. At low speed only a small amount of mixture goes to the cylinders, so only a small amount of fumes passes through. At high speed much more fuel mixture flows to the cylinders, and the PCV valve admits more fumes.

Quick-checking. Begin by quick-checking the system. Look for the hose from the air-cleaner housing to the engine and disconnect it from the engine (Fig. 8-15). On some cars it goes to the oil fill cap on the top cover—in this case, just remove the cap.

Place a sheet of paper over the opening in the valve cover (Fig. 8-16). With the engine idling, a light vacuum should hold the piece of paper in place. If it does not, locate the PCV valve. It will be in or at one end of a hose from another part of the engine top cover to the base of the carburetor. Or on a V-type engine (V-6, V-8, etc.), the hose may be connected to the other engine top cover.

8-15.   Disconnecting the fresh-air inlet at engine top cover.

8-16.   Checking for light vacuum by holding a piece of paper over the fresh-air inlet.

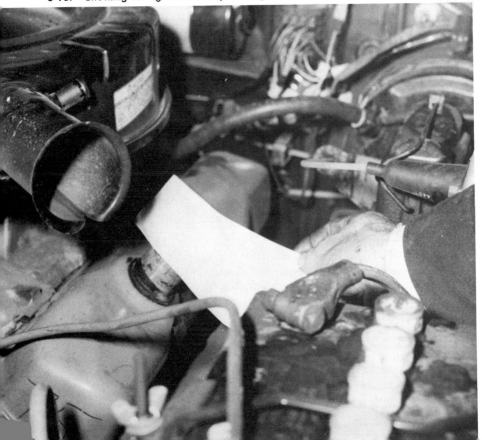

8-17. This PCV valve in a grommet in the engine top cover is obvious and accessible.

With the engine off, disconnect the valve from the hose or pull it (on its hose) from the engine top cover (see Figs. 8-17, 8-18). Shake the valve and you should hear a jiggling noise, indicating the working parts inside are free. If you don't replace the valve.

8-18. This PCV valve in the hose from the engine to the carburetor base was hidden.

8-19. Feeling the end of the PCV valve for a vacuum with the engine idling. If there is no vacuum, the valve is plugged and should be replaced.

8-20. PCV fresh-air filter in air cleaner is easily removed. Just pry up the clip with the screwdriver and pull it out. On other cars the filter can be pulled out of the holder.

If you hear the jiggling, proceed to this second test. Start the engine and put your finger over the disconnected end of the hose, or the end of the valve. You should feel a vacuum (Fig. 8-19). If there is none, either the hose or the valve is plugged. Remove both and check the hose with a piece of wire. If it's clear, replace the valve.

PCV air cleaner. Whenever, you service the air cleaner or the PCV valve, inspect the little PCV air filter (if it is used) and replace it if it is dirty. On some cars the filter is just a piece of foam or fiber that can be pulled out of its little holder. On others the filter and holder are retained by a clip. Just pry up the clip and remove the holder assembly through the inside of the air-cleaner housing (Fig. 8-20).

If the extra filter is not used, the PCV design may supply clean air from the inside of the air filter housing, in which case the regular air filter is doing double duty. As a result, the filter may have somewhat shorter life.

AUTOMATIC CHOKE. The automatic choke does exactly what the name says: it automatically chokes off the air supply when the engine is cold. Reducing the air content in the fuel mixture makes the engine easier to start and run when cold.

The choke is a plate that fits into the top of the carburetor, where it is mounted on a shaft that permits it to pivot (Fig. 8-21). The shaft is connected by linkage to a temperature-sensitive coil spring.

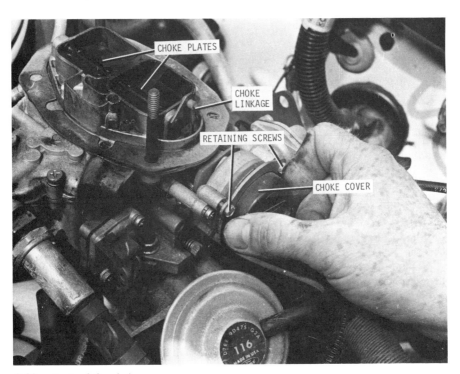

8-21. Parts of the choke.

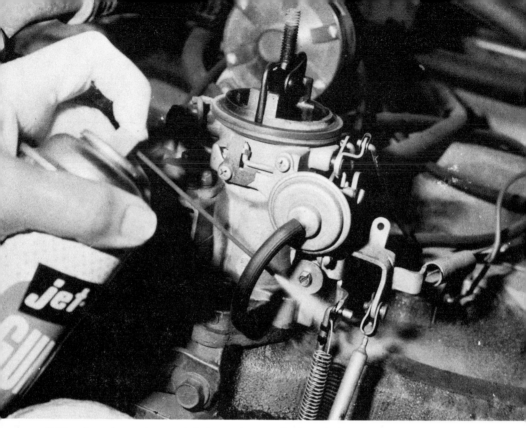

8-22. Spraying carburetor linkages with aerosol solvent helps keep them working freely.

When the engine is cold, the spring winds tightly together and pivots the choke plate to a horizontal position, restricting the air supply that can get through the carburetor. As the engine warms up, the coil unwinds and the choke plate is pulled to the vertical position, so the maximum amount of air can flow past it.

To make sure the choke does its job, spray the plate, the shaft on which it is mounted, and the linkage to which it is connected with penetrating solvent (Fig. 8-22). Do not oil the linkage, for oil can make the linkage surfaces sticky and dirt will adhere, eventually interfering with choke operation.

Choke adjustment. Many chokes are easily adjusted, if necessary, by a weekend mechanic. To determine if yours is a type you can adjust, see if the carburetor has a circular plastic cover (Fig. 8-21). Inside that cover (and attached to it) is the choke's temperature-sensitive coil.

To determine if adjustment is necessary, floor the gas pedal with the engine off and release. If the engine is cold, the plate should pivot and close off the top of the carburetor. If it doesn't, pivot the plate back and forth with your fingers to be sure it operates freely. If there's any binding, the source of the bind must be found and corrected. Perhaps it's just a burr on a linkage joint or dirt on the linkage.

If the choke plate can be moved easily back and forth, but doesn't close completely when the engine is cold, it can be adjusted. First, check a specifications manual for automatic choke setting, which will be "INDEX" or a certain number of marks in the "RICH" direction (such as 2R, which means two marks in the rich direction). Next, slacken the cover-retaining screws (Fig. 8-21) and turn the cover in whichever direction causes the plate to close off the top of the carburetor. If you encounter difficulty, press the gas pedal to the floor once more to make sure that the gas pedal linkage has disengaged fully from the choke. Also, be sure you are starting with a cold engine, one that has not been started in at least six hours.

Once the choke plate is closed, keep turning the cover until its single mark lines up with the center mark on the carburetor body (Fig. 8-23). That center mark is "INDEX." If the specification calls for a number of marks in the rich direction, continue to turn the cover in the same direction until the single mark on the cover lines up with the specified mark on the body. Hold the cover in position and tighten the retaining screws.

Note: On some carburetors there is a single mark on the carburetor body and the series of marks is on the cover. The adjustment procedure is the same.

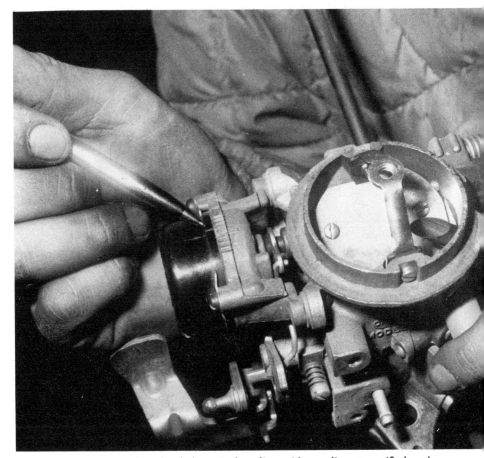

8-23. Pen points to mark on the choke cover that aligns with an adjacent specified mark on the carburetor body.

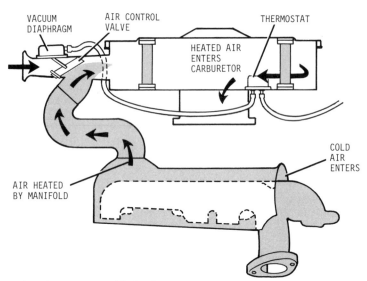

8-24. When the engine is cold, the thermostatic air cleaner draws in hot air through a duct from the exhaust manifold. When the engine is warm, a flap blocks off the preheat duct and admits cooler air through the normal opening.

THERMOSTATIC AIR CLEANER. Virtually all late-model cars have what is called a thermostatic air cleaner. The air cleaner housing has its normal opening for the entry of air, plus a second one at the bottom (Fig. 8-24), to which is connected a duct that attaches to the exterior of the exhaust system.

When the cold engine is first started, the hot exhaust gases inside will instantly heat up the exhaust system. The air adjacent to the exhaust system is also warmed, and the duct that covers the system becomes a source of warm air.

Warm air helps to break up the fuel mixture into vapor, which will burn more readily. To help the engine until it warms up and can heat the air as it passes through the carburetor and intake manifold, the duct system supplies preheated air. To prevent cold air from entering, a flap inside the air cleaner assembly pivots to block off the normal opening.

When the engine warms up and can heat the air within the carburetor and intake manifold, the flap then pivots, closing off the duct from the exhaust system and opening the normal passage to admit cold air. The system is controlled by engine vacuum through a temperature-sensitive device in the air cleaner housing (see Fig. 8-25).

If the flap sticks in either the preheated air or the cold air position, problems will result. If the flap stays in the heat-off position, the engine will stumble and stall when cold. If it sticks in the preheat air position, the air coming into the air cleaner will be overheated when the engine is warmed up, and the engine will suffer loss of power.

To check, with the engine idling determine where the flap is when the engine is cold and when it is hot. On most cars you can reach inside the air cleaner opening with your fingers (Fig. 8-26) or a screwdriver. On others (Figs. 8-27 and 8-28.) you may have to disconnect a section of the air cleaner to be able to see or reach into the part with the flap.

8-25. Temperature-sensitive device in the air cleaner controls vacuum diaphragm, which operates the flap.

8-26. On some cars the position of the flap can be checked with the fingers.

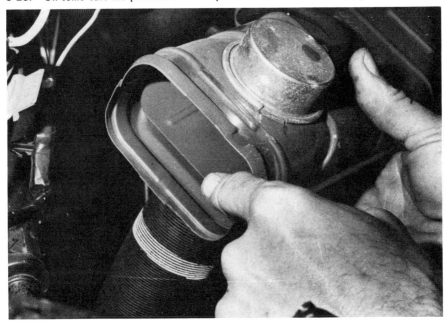

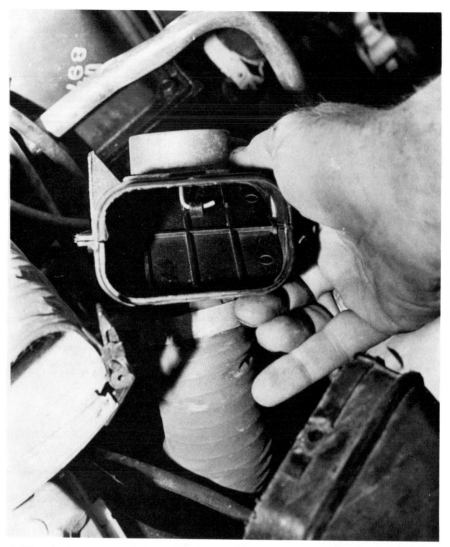

8-27. The flap on this car is in a section of the air cleaner that must be disconnected for inspection. Note that the flap is closing off the normal opening of the air cleaner, permitting the engine to draw warm air from the preheat duct. This is for cold engine operation

If the flap is stuck in the wrong position, determine if it can be moved easily. If it stays in the wrong position with the engine on, but moves easily back and forth with the engine off, the problem is in the thermostatic control, and replacing it is a job for a professional mechanic. If the flap is just sticky, spray the shaft with penetrating solvent.

HEAT CONTROL VALVE. The engine has another device to warm up the air, and this one works by heating up the intake manifold, the series of chambers that carry fuel mixture from the carburetor to the cylinders. The device, called a manifold heat-control valve, or heat riser, is a flap valve that directs exhaust gases in either of two ways. On a V-engine it opens or closes an exhaust gas passage through the intake manifold. On an in-line engine, such as a 4 or 6 cylinder, it directs the gases against the top of the exhaust manifold, which butts against the bottom of the intake manifold.

The heat riser has an external thermostatic coil, mounted very close to the exhaust manifold, so it responds to changes in temperature (Fig. 8-29). When the coil is cold, it closes up and pivots the valve into the heat-on position. When the coil gets hot (as the engine warms up), it unwinds and pivots the valve into the heat-off position. A sticking valve has basically the same effect as the sticking flap in a thermostatic air cleaner.

To determine if your engine is equipped with this device, look at the exhaust manifold (both of them on the sides of a V-type engine) and see if there is a counterweight and coil on the exterior (Fig. 8-29), at the point where all the branches come together into a single section.

8-28. Engine is warmed up and idling, and so flap pivots to shut off the preheat duct and allow cooler air through the normal opening.

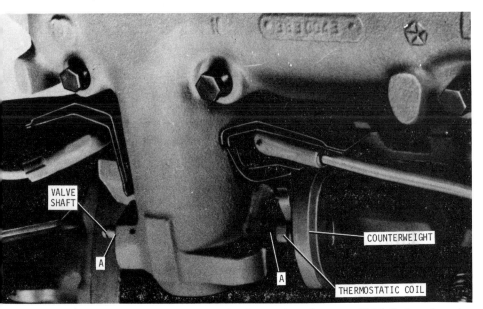

8-29. This is the manifold heat-control valve on the exhaust manifold. To free the valve when it is stuck, spray penetrating solvent at points A.

Grasp the counterweight and try to flip it back and forth. If it sticks even slightly, spray penetrating solvent into both sides of the hole in the manifold in which the valve's shaft is mounted. Work the counterweight back and forth until the device pivots freely. *Note:* If it's badly stuck, you may have to tap the counterweight with a hammer until the solvent works in and frees the device.

The location of the heat riser may force you to work underneath with the car supported on safety stands.

9 | Emergency Repairs

Almost anything can happen to electrical and mechanical systems, and the automobile has so many of each that the possibility of an emergency failure always exists. If you take care of your car, however, the chances of an inopportune breakdown will be reduced.

When a road emergency occurs, there is a practical limit to what you should be ready to attempt. Yes, there are the grown-up Boy Scout types—always prepared with a trunk full of tools and parts, and willing to spend the better part of a day or more tackling a medium-to-heavy repair, working on the shoulder of a road. This is unrealistic. It makes a lot more sense to check your car periodically, do what is needed in the convenience of your garage or driveway, than to load up the trunk and wait for a breakdown.

This chapter will cover common emergencies that you can do something about very quickly, with just a few basic tools you can put into a small box—pliers, screwdrivers, a few wrenches, battery booster cables, a roll of wire, plastic electrical tape, and a hand siphon pump.

CAR WON'T START. A starting failure is the most common problem, so let's look at the simplest causes.

Engine doesn't crank. Check the battery for water; if it's low, add water until the level is above the tops of the plates inside. Inspect the battery cable connections at both ends. If they're corroded, remove them and clean them with a screwdriver. Then flag down a good samaritan and boost-start the engine with the cables.

Engine cranks but won't start. There are many possibilities, but only two common causes you might be able to do something about quickly: flooding or closed ignition points (on cars without electronic ignition).

To determine if the problem is caused by too much fuel "flooding" out the engine, try to start it with the gas pedal pressed firmly to the floor. Crank, and if the engine seems to be about to start, flooding may be the problem. A strong odor of gas under the hood is another indication. Wait ten to fifteen minutes for the fuel in the engine to evaporate, then try again with the gas pedal pressed to the floor.

To determine if you have an ignition problem, make a simple check for spark to the plugs by disconnecting a spark-plug wire at the plug and holding it 1/8 inch from a metal section of the engine. If the plug wire terminal is recessed in a rubber nipple, stuff a metal object (such as a key) into it, something that will project from the nipple, as shown in Fig. 9-1. Hold the plug wire so the metal projection is 1/8 inch from the engine metal.

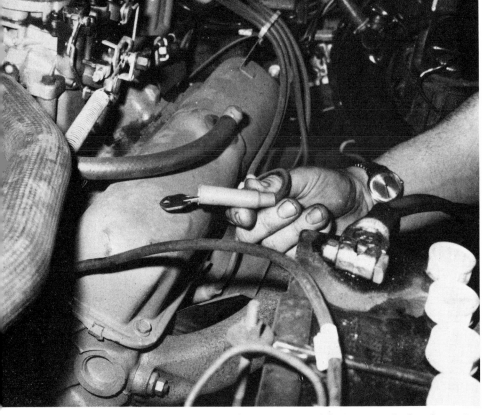

9-1. Insert a key in a plug wire terminal so you can see if there is a spark when the engine is cranked. Keep the key 1/8 inch from the electrical ground—the metal engine. If the nipple is deteriorated, tie a handkerchief around it to avoid getting a shock.

Have someone crank the engine. You should see an uninterrupted series of sparks jumping across the gap to the engine—at least one spark every two to three seconds. If you don't see sparks, or if they are sporadic, you have an ignition system problem, possibly closed ignition points. *Caution:* if the nipple is deteriorated, prevent the possibility of an electric shock when making this test by wrapping a piece of cloth around the plug wire near the end and hold the cloth, not the wire itself.

Next, remove the distributor cap and look at the points while someone cranks the engine. You should see the points open and close a tiny fraction of an inch, over and over, as the engine is cranked. If they don't open, you've found the problem.

You can adjust the breaker points using a matchbook cover as an emergency feeler gauge. If you don't have a wrench to slacken the distributor lock and turn the distributor, use the short-burst-cranking method explained in Chapter 7.

LOCKED OUT. Locking yourself out of your car is embarrassing, but you're not the first person to whom it happens and you won't be the last. If you can obtain a coat hanger and a nail file, you may be able to save the situation.

Straighten the coat-hanger wire and form one end into a U-shaped hook. If you have a nail file, run it along the inside surface of the hook to roughen it up, which will improve its grip.

Force the wire into the car between door frame and molding, and guide the hook end onto the door lock knob, just below the point where the vertical surface mushrooms (Fig. 9-2). Pull up on the wire; if you're lucky the knob will come up. You may have to try a number of times but eventually you should be able to raise the knob.

Note: On two-door Ford cars since 1977 the door knobs, when pushed down, are flush with the top of the door (an anti-theft measure), and this technique will not work.

An alternate method that may be easier is to extract the keys that you left inside the car. If you don't have them on a thick holder, which will not pass between door frame and molding, this technique is worth a try. The keys may be on the seat or still in the ignition-start switch. In the latter case, the key must be in the extreme counterclockwise position in order to come out.

Still another possibility is pulling the door handle with the wire. On many cars you don't have to pull the handle all the way; just a partial movement will automatically raise the door knob.

With either of these methods, which involve working from the right side of the car, a single coat hanger may not provide enough wire. You may have to splice two hangers together.

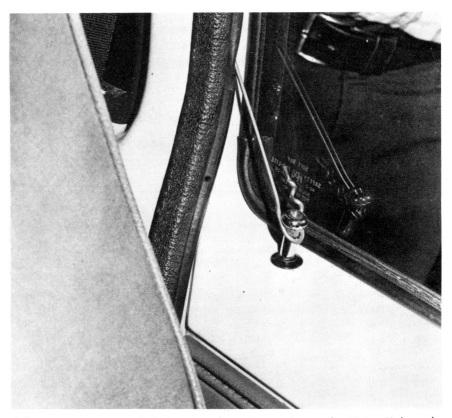

9-2. Easy way to enter a locked car is to slip a wire coat hanger, bent into a U-shape, between the frame and molding, and release the lock knob.

OUT OF GAS. Gas gauges aren't accurate and running out of gas is one of the most common road emergencies. There are three ways to minimize the distress.

1. Keep a pint of carburetor solvent in the glove box. The carburetor solvent may not keep the engine running satisfactorily all by itself, but it will mix with the small amount of gas that remains in a tank when the engine stalls and get you going again. A pint is only 1/8 of a gallon, but that might be enough to get you to a gas station.

2. Keep an empty gas can in the trunk. If you can get someone to give you a lift to a station, at least you won't face a problem if the station doesn't have a can, or if the station is out of the way you are going and requires a security deposit for the can.

3. Keep a liquid siphon in your toolbox. A plastic, hand-operated liquid siphon costs less than $1 and if you can get some gas from a good samaritan, you could be on your way very quickly.

HEADLAMPS OUT. A sudden, complete headlamp failure is rarely caused by burnout of the sealed beams. The typical system, whether two or four eyes, will generally suffer only one filament burnout at a time, giving you sufficient opportunity to obtain a replacement.

When both (or four) eyes are extinguished simultaneously, there are two likely possibilities: failure of the dimmer switch or the headlamp switch.

If the dimmer switch is the problem, it might just be sticking. Try punching the button with your foot ten or fifteen times; if the lights finally come on, you've found the problem. Have the switch replaced as soon as possible.

If the lights don't come on, the dimmer switch may have failed completely or the headlamp switch is at fault. Rather than go through a complex troubleshooting sequence, make an emergency repair with a piece of wire and the plastic electrical tape.

First, gain access to a headlamp's wire connector. You may be able to do this by raising the hood of the car and working through the engine compartment, or by turning the wheel out and working through the fender opening. If neither is easy, remove the molding and retaining ring from the headlamp itself, as explained in Chapter 5.

There are three sets of wires at each connector for a two-headlamp system (one set for high beams, one for low and one for electrical ground). There are two sets of wires (one for the beam, one for ground) on cars with four eyes.

Pick a headlamp connector wire that doesn't have a black insulating jacket (that's for electrical ground) and with a knife or razor blade, strip away about a quarter to half-inch of insulation somewhere along the length of the wire. Remove an inch or so of insulation from the end of the roll wire and splice it to the bared section of headlamp connector wire. Then tape over the splice.

Run the roll wire to the car battery and connect it to the battery's starter terminal. Just slacken the cable retaining nut or bolt, cut the wire from the roll, strip an inch or so of insulation from the end and wrap it around the threads. Then tighten the connection.

The headlamps should go on. On a two-lamp system you may get the high beams or the low beams, but at least you'll have lights. To shut off the lights, disconnect the wire from the battery.

EMERGENCY KIT. Many weekend mechanics like to keep an assortment of spare parts in the trunk. Actually, beyond those items outlined in this chapter, very few of those things you might consider storing would ever be used in an emergency.

You could keep a set of ignition points, for example, but the usual problem is closing of the points. Even if inspection shows the points are badly burned, a quick cleaning of the contact faces with a nail file will usually get the car started. It may not run well or for long, but filing on the road and replacing when at home is a simpler approach.

Radiator hoses are also popular "emergency box" items, and you probably can't go wrong keeping a set in your car. However, if any hose starts to leak badly, you can probably get away with wrapping it with plastic electrical tape. It may still leak, but you should be able to cut down the leakage sufficiently to get home or to a service station. Wrapping with tape is a lot faster than trying to change a hose, particularly many heater and lower radiator hoses.

Got a leak? There are emergency sealants, but for unpressurized systems, such as oil and gas, chewing gum (well-chewed) is a useful temporary seal.

If a drive belt snaps and your alternator light comes on, you might want to do an immediate repair. But there's enough reserve capacity in the typical battery (at or near full charge on a moderately warm day) to drive for up to an hour or more. Turn off the radio and heater or air conditioning to conserve electricity, and drive at a moderate, steady speed so the engine doesn't overheat. The belt that runs the alternator also operates the fan and water pump on most cars.

Yes, installing a new belt you have in the trunk can be done, but on some cars the job could be a real struggle on a highway shoulder and really require tools you don't have with you. There are emergency fan belt kits you can wrap around the pulleys and install in minutes, but in a pinch you also could make a drive belt out of clothesline.

A variation of Murphy's Law says that if you load up your car with replacements for all the things that normally would go wrong, something for which you aren't prepared will happen. Your best bets for road emergencies are to check your car periodically at home and get to know it better. The more you know about your car, the more likely you are to be able to use your brain (the best tool of all) and think of a solution, no matter what the problem.

Index